The ET Visitor's Guide to the U.S.A.

A Satire

Leonard Feinberg

Pilgrims' Process, Inc., Boulder, CO

This is a work of fiction. All characters and events portrayed in this book are either products of the author's imagination or are used fictitiously.

THE ET VISITOR'S GUIDE TO THE U.S.A.

Copyright © 2002 by Pilgrims' Process, Inc.

ISBN: 0-9710609-2-4

Library of Congress Control Number: 2001095531

Printed in the United States of America

0 9 8 7 6 5 4 3 2 1

Preface

The manuscript for this book came into my possession totally unexpectedly. A professor of psychiatry at my university introduced me to a man whom he was treating for amnesia. The man was ordinary looking, about thirty years old, well dressed and in possession of a large sum of cash. My colleague explained that the man could not remember where he had come from but thought his name was Aleshker. Since my wife and I had a large house and our children had already left home, the psychiatrist suggested that we let Aleshker live with us, as a paying guest, while he recuperated. We agreed.

Aleshker turned out to be a pleasant person, polite, intelligent, and extremely inquisitive. He asked questions about every aspect of American life, and he seemed to remember, in photographic and phonographic detail, everything that he saw, heard, or read while he lived with us. Since he never recalled what his first name was, we called him Al.

We took him everywhere we went: parties, the theater, opera, sports events. Everywhere he was observant and everywhere politely curious. And he read, quickly and intently, everything from Plato to Superman comics.

Aleksher had a dry wit, quiet and understated. As an outsider he saw things differently and commented on them with a wry sense of humor. Not everyone appreciated it.

Soon after he moved in he asked permission to use my computer to record the progress of his recovery. Every day he spent several hours at the computer, especially toward the end of his stay with us.

Six months after he arrived, Al told us that he finally remembered; he had come from New York, he said, and he was ready to return there. He bade us a friendly good-bye, took with him the computer disks he had used, and departed.

When I next used the computer I realized that, without Al's knowledge, a hard-disc copy of all his work was still in the computer. I tried to trace him in New York, unsuccessfully. He seems to have disappeared.

Aleshker is apparently under the delusion that he is an extraterrestrial being. But his manuscript, written from a quite different perspective than that of American sociologists, may be of interest to what Aleshker calls "Earthlings."

Leonard Feinberg

Introduction

Of all the creatures that inhabit the planet Earth the ones that call themselves human beings are the most interesting to study. They consider themselves superior to all other species, although an insect called the cockroach existed long before humans appeared and will probably survive after they are gone.

The extraterrestrial visitor to the planet Earth must understand that human society operates by balancing the desires of the individual (which are basically selfish) against the needs of society (which are beneficial to that particular society).

Similarly, the individual human being functions by balancing his or her need to achieve pleasant survival (which requires competitive behavior) against his or her desire to be loved or admired (which causes kindly deeds).

The most pervasive characteristic of human beings that I have observed is controlled aggression. In some people this tendency toward contention is largely suppressed, in others it is openly expressed. No matter what you hear about the prevalence of brotherly love, don't count on it if you have no money.

One final word of caution: Don't believe everything that Earthlings tell you. It may, or may not, be the truth.

One

Physique

The extraterrestrial visitor should not laugh at the physical appearance of human beings. Their shapes certainly are ridiculous, but they can't help it.

By the standards of our galaxy the construction of the human body is grotesque. At the top is a roundish part called the head. The brain, inside the human head, directs the behavior of geniuses and fools, considerably more of the latter than the former. The brain thinks, remembers, rationalizes, and devises all sorts of strategies for survival, pleasure, and outmaneuvering the competition. It also suggests witty remarks an hour or two after the opportunity to make these remarks has passed.

Although this brain is responsible for the success of the species, it has less control of human actions than emotions do. The attempt to account for this has wasted a lot of intellectuals' time.

In front of the head is a face, on which are two eyes that provide vision. The female eye is especially adept at seeing bargains in printed advertisements, on television, and at garage sales. The male eye keeps looking for pretty women. Human eyes are incredibly adaptable. They permit people to see what they want to see, and not to see what they don't want to see.

Ears—two organs, one on each side of the head—are equally adjustable. Through them human beings hear what they want to hear and fail to hear what they don't want to hear. The female ear is particularly attuned to gossip, especially about sexual indiscretions and other trivia. The male ear thrives on the latest scores of athletic events. The ears of young Americans accept, voluntarily, excruciating cacophonies of noise called rock-and-roll music.

In the middle of the face is the nose, a small organ used for breathing, for localizing colds, for smelling flowers when the owner of the nose has time to smell flowers, and for looking down one's nose at people who have shorter or longer noses.

Just below the nose is the mouth, an orifice that takes in food and ejects sounds. It is a very skillful instrument, used both to inform and to deceive, delivering both messages with the same apparent sincerity.

Inside the mouth are teeth, white, bone-like structures arranged in rows, used for biting and chewing food. Human beings have devised many additional methods of biting adversaries, without using teeth.

It is hard for the ET visitor to realize how important the features of the human face are to human beings. A nose that is an inch longer than average may condemn a person to lifelong ridicule. Floppy ears give people inferiority complexes. Eyes a little too close together, or a little too far apart, may diminish a person's social life.

To avoid these dismal possibilities many human beings embellish their physical characteristics with extraneous devices. Most Americans improve their vision by wearing glasses or contacts, the latter a means of concealing the wearer's need for visual aid. Many older Americans wear hearing aids, also trying to conceal the presence of the aid. Vanity seems to be the only reason for pretending that the aid is not present.

When the hair on top of their heads thins or disappears, many Americans put on wigs and hairpieces. When their teeth fall out, Americans replace them with false teeth. What the ET visitor sees may not be the real thing. In some cases it is a greatly embellished imitation.

Below the head is an elongated torso, to which two arms and two legs are attached. Locomotion is achieved by movement of the legs, often more rapidly than is necessary because Americans are always in a hurry to get somewhere. The destination is rarely worth the extra effort.

The two arms are limbs extending from the shoulder to the hand. The part of the arm below the wrist is called the hand and is used for grasping, fondling, and shooting. Male American hands are particularly adept at handling guns, fishing rods, golf clubs, and bowling balls. Judging from television commercials, American women use their hands mostly for comparing laundry detergents.

Hands are also a rich source of communication and deception. They are used for sending messages by handwritten or typewritten note, or by computer and fax machine and other devices. Americans constantly send messages. And, as with the spoken word, all these messages seem equally truthful, even when many of them are in fact distortions of the truth, perversions of the truth, and outright lies.

Protruding from the middle of many adult torsos is a large glob of fat called the stomach. A large part of the nation's gross income depends on sales of medications for everything from mild indigestion to bleeding ulcers inside the stomach.

Humans exist by ingesting, digesting, and excreting food. They say that God and country are very important—but food comes first.

Ambrose Bierce, an American writer, described the diaphragm as "a muscular partition separating diseases of the chest from diseases of the bowels." But for most Americans that definition is not accurate—until they reach middle age.

Inside the torso beats the heart, a hollow muscular organ that circulates the blood in human creatures. Although the heart is traditionally assumed to be the source of love and compassion, many heartless people seem to function very successfully.

In the United States, a symmetrical arrangement of eyes, ears, nose, and mouth is considered beautiful—though the expression is often bovine. A thin figure is considered desirable, though few Americans are thin. And a general air of cheerful friendliness is typical of the American who has a home, a job, and a cellular telephone.

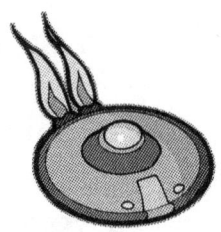

Two

The Sexes

Unlike the inhabitants of our galaxy, human beings have differences in physical structure that identify them as males or females. Females have vaginas, in which the reproductive process begins, and breasts, through which a few American infants feed themselves. Males have frankfurter-like appendages called penises, which eject the sperm necessary to fertilize the female. The penis hangs from the bottom of the torso, in front.

Freudian psychoanalysts claim that some women suffer from "penis envy." Sallie Tisdale denigrates the term by defining it as a "a desire to be red, wrinkled, and four inches long."

In the United States women live, on the average, seven years longer than men. Whether this is a reward or a punishment is uncertain. And American women are endowed with an extra chromosome that compels them to go shopping whenever they have a spare moment.

In every society on Earth the jobs held by women pay less than the jobs held by men. Since men and women are supposedly equal, the explanation for the disparity must be that women prefer lower wages. Male chauvinism, men claim, has nothing to do with the case. It just happens that way.

Although anthropologists classify a few cultures as "matriarchal" (female rule), most social scientists believe that "patriarchy" (male governance) is much more common. Actually, women rule everywhere indirectly by controlling their husbands and children, but it is considered impolite to mention this fact.

A survey of American society in 1991, in a book called *Day of Truth*, concluded that women are morally superior to men, more responsible, and more honest in the workplace. But the English writer Rudyard Kipling called the female of the species more deadly than the male.

More anti-female than anti-male epigrams have been recorded. "Woman was God's second mistake," wrote Friedrich Nietzche, a German misogynist. American educator Nicholas Butler was also cynical: "Brigands demand your money or your life; women require both."

"Women will probably be the last animal civilized by man," wrote English novelist George Meredith. Judging from man's behavior, man is hardly qualified to do much civilizing.

Florence Kennedy, an American feminist, says, "If men bore children, there would be no anti-abortion laws."

Ambrose Bierce defined the word "his" as "hers." Women call him "Bitter Bierce"; men do not.

What in previous ages was called promiscuity is now described by the euphemism "sexual freedom."

In ancient China a proverb advised, "Curse not your wife in the evening, or you will have to sleep alone." In Buddhist Sri Lanka a popular witticism says, "The ex-priest atoned for his previous celibacy by taking two wives."

Defending concubinage in the nineteenth century, Chinese wit Ku Hung-Wing wrote, "Whereas you always see a teapot with four cups, you never find a teacup with four teapots."

And Jorge Luis Borges, an Argentinian writer, made a typically Borgesian comment: "Mirrors and copulation are abominable because they increase the number of men."

In spite of all the talk about the power of sex, a recent survey claimed 15% of Americans preferred watching television to having sex.

Love, in the form of a powerful attraction between two human beings, seems to be one of the few human activities that is not measured by cost-effectiveness.

Since the spread of AIDS, ET visitors to the Earth are advised not to experiment with human sexual intercourse, even for the sake of science, without taking proper precautions.

Three

Types

Recently, some physicians have divided human beings into three types: aggressive, depressed, and well adjusted. All three types, the doctors discovered, eventually die.

According to Russian philosopher G. I. Gurdjieff's theory of the Enneagram, there are nine types of human beings: The Perfectionist, the Helper, the Achiever, the Romantic, the Observer, the Questioner, the Adventurer, the Asserter, and the Peacemaker. They all die also.

At large corporations personnel directors use special criteria in evaluating employees. These criteria always prove that the personnel directors themselves are eminently fitted for their jobs.

In another unsuccessful attempt, English satirist Aldous Huxley proposed a method of categorizing people: ectomorphs (thin, introverted), endomorphs (fat, lazy, soft), and mesomorphs (muscular, aggressive). But ectomorphs like Huxley invented the nuclear bomb; with a phone in his hand an endomorph can be very energetic; and in real life many mesomorphs fail to conform to the formula.

In ancient times people believed that everyone is dominated by one of four parts of the body called humours—blood, phlegm, black bile and yellow bile. In those days there seemed to be an excessive number of people controlled by black bile, which was believed to cause melancholy.

Introverts and extroverts, dominating persons and submissive ones, activists and pacifists, mystics and materialists—there are more types, ad infinitum.

There seem to be two kinds of people—those who manage to succeed in any environment and the remaining majority, lost and baffled.

In spite of efforts to classify people by type, every American thinks of himself or herself as a unique individual, stumbling through or enjoying life in his or her own unpredictable way.

Four

Heredity and Environment

Human scholars spend an inordinate amount of time debating the issue of heredity versus environment, or nature versus nurture.

Social biologists are convinced that it is genes rather than society that account for the brilliance of social biologists and the stupidity of other scholars. But other social scientists insist that it is the environment that has the greater influence in shaping human beings—aided, of course, by the superior intelligence of social scientists.

Human beings have concocted three theories to explain why they behave as they do. The first is the *tabula rasa* (clean slate) concept. It assumes that humans are born as totally pliable creatures whose environment determines whether they become a scientist like Albert Einstein, a comedian like Charlie Chaplin, or a monster like Joseph Stalin.

The second theory is that human beings are born evil and only a strict society can force them to behave in a socially acceptable manner. Both religious fundamentalist John Calvin and atheist Sigmund Freud accept the inherent iniquity of humanity. (Many Christian sects attribute this wicked characteristic to the sin Adam and Eve committed in the Garden of Eden. The location of this Garden has not been completely verified.)

Contradicting this notion of inherent evil is the third theory: Human beings are born good but are forced to behave badly by the society in which they live. Presumably it was this bad society that made French philosopher Jean-Jacques Rousseau, the most famous proponent of this idea, abandon all five of his children to orphan homes.

Scientists who disagree with other scientists minimize the evidence of their opponents and exaggerate the data that support their own position. This is called the scientific method.

Recently several scientists discovered what they call the "selfish" gene. It (call it Cain) kills its brother chromosome (call it Abel) in order to monopolize the next generation and thrive at the expense of Abel. Scientist Richard Dawkins believes that all human beings carry a selfish gene that makes them act in egotistic ways, always protecting their own interests at the expense of other persons.

Another scientist suggests that human beings also carry an "altruistic" gene that, at times, makes them behave benevolently. There seem to be more selfish genes than altruistic genes around.

Although no biologist has yet identified a "lazy" gene among human beings, there is abundant evidence for its existence.

If genius is not transmitted by genes it is hard to explain five-year-old musicians like Wolfgang A. Mozart and seven-year-old mathematicians like Blaise Pascal.

Five

Race

The most obvious division of human beings, after gender, is race.

In their basic nature and latent talents, human beings seem to be very much alike, all over the world. But an extraterrestrial visitor would be making a very grave mistake if he assumed that human beings themselves think they are alike.

Each of the races thinks that there is something abnormal about the other races.

Some of this racial prejudice may stem from poor eyesight. Many Occidentals say, "All Orientals look the same to me." And Asians have been heard to say, "All white people look alike to me."

During a recent war, American soldiers called Vietnamese people "slant-eyes." Japanese children insult Caucasians in their midst by calling them "round-eyes."

It is an amusing irony that millions of white people spend innumerable hours tanning themselves in the sun and under ultraviolet lamps, in order to look darker. And some Black people use whitening cream on their faces to look lighter.

Nor is this kind of prejudice limited to human beings. A Polish farmer used to catch crows, paint them with white limewater, and then release them. He enjoyed watching black crows attack the painted bird.

Racial prejudices increase the self-esteem of all groups—from primitive Zulus to sophisticated Frenchmen. Slight differences in physical characteristics seem to be enough to arouse hostility and contempt among human beings. Earthlings tend to have friendly feelings about people like themselves and prejudice toward those who seem different.

The most bitter hostilities keep occurring between groups that are very similar to each other, such as French Catholics and French Protestants, Irish Catholics and Irish Protestants, Muslim Sunnis and Muslim Shiites, African Tutsis and African Hutus, Arab Semites and Hebrew Semites, and so on.

Anthropologists' diagnoses of barbaric behavior do remarkably little to comfort the victims of barbaric behavior. By the end of the "civilized" twentieth century ethnocentrism flourished on a larger and more violent scale than ever before.

In every country minority groups complain of discrimination against them. In every country, their complaints are valid. And in every multilingual country the different languages have strengthened the feeling of separateness, not the mirage of unity.

Every large group and nation needs some minority to despise or hate. Jews have been obliging enough, by being minorities in many parts of the world, to provide an object of hatred in places where no other group is available.

In deteriorating economies people who are "different" quickly become scapegoats.

A few years ago sociologist Emory Bogardus analyzed the attitudes of people in the United States toward the ethnic minorities in the country. The list, in descending order of respect: English, Scottish, Canadian, French, Dutch, Swedish, German, Italians, Poles, Czechs, Greeks, Jews, Blacks, Turks, Chinese, and Koreans. The people of each ethnic group declared their own group the one most worthy of approval.

Heredity stamps each person with a racial and ethnic identity that that person can never escape.

In India there is an anecdote about the creation of man that has a charming ethnic rationalization. When God first experimented with making man, He put a clay figure into the kiln. But He pulled it out too soon, and the figure came out colored white. God tried again, but He was interrupted during the firing and by the time He belatedly took the figure out of the kiln it was black. So God tried once more. This time He gauged the process carefully and achieved the perfect result—a brown man.

Six

Aging

For the young, life offers an infinite variety of new pleasures. For the old, life offers an infinite variety of new pains.

While the old enjoy pleasures slightly, they suffer pains intensely.

Extending human longevity is a mixed blessing. Many old people have only the past to look forward to.

In the year 1600 old age was thought to begin at thirty. In 1600 it also, frequently, ended there.

The elderly members of every generation consider all social change a change for the worse. Today's elderly people consider currently popular music an abominable concatenation of irritating noises, forgetting that the popular music of their own youth was just as objectionable to older men and women.

Nothing is what it used to be, the elderly like to say.

As they grow older some people change from having nothing to say, to saying it repeatedly.

Many older people have animal pets. They sustain that relationship more skillfully than they manage the companionship of relatives and other adults.

Monomania about trifles seems to inject purpose into the lives of some senior citizens. When there are no big problems to worry about, elderly people tend to be inordinately disturbed by little things.

The elderly say, quite reasonably, that most of what they forgot was not worth remembering.

In retirement communities, by the time a statement has gone through three hearing aids, it is rarely the original statement.

If poet T. S. Eliot's character J. Alfred Prufrock lived to old age, he would measure out his life not in coffee spoons but in bowel movements.

Many young people are unhappy because they don't know who they are. Some older people are unhappy because they do know who they are.

On the other hand, the English poet Robert Browning wrote, "Come, grow old with me / The best is yet to be."

And the French writer George Sand wrote to Gustave Flaubert: "Before long, you will gradually be entering upon the happiest part of life: old age."

Italians have a recipe for happiness: "Good health, love, wealth—and the time to enjoy them." For those elderly people who meet these requirements, life can be very pleasant.

Seven

Death

It is not death itself that many people fear so much as the manner of dying. A long terminal illness is what most of the elderly dread.

The infirmities of old age, the indignities of decline, the absurdity of senility make death a more acceptable prospect for the old than it is for the young.

The able person who does not fear death has unique advantages and opportunities.

In an ancient Roman novel, *The Satyricon,* the wealthy Trimalchio hired a trumpeter to blow every hour as a reminder to Trimalchio that he had one hour less to live. Today people tear off the pages of the calendar. It is less expensive.

American filmmaker Woody Allen said, "I am not afraid of dying but I would rather be somewhere else when it happens."

In India people believe that the city of Varanasi is the luckiest place to die. The Nepalese prefer a certain temple in Katmandu, which is geographically more convenient for Nepalese.

Ancient Egyptians and East Indians hired professional weepers for funerals. Modern Chinese hire professional entertainers.

The funeral procession is the only assemblage of automobiles (besides political dignitaries and wedding parties) permitted to ignore stoplights on the way to its destination.

There is a rumor that the more luxuriant cruise lines, when they perform burials at sea, put an American Express card into the shrouds. Just in case, I suppose.

There is more lying done in funeral eulogies than in most other formal statements—except for political speeches.

Although American satirist Mark Twain said that the only happy people were the mad and the dead, he himself lived as long as he could.

And English writer George Bernard Shaw said that the will to live was inexplicable, but he delayed dying until he was ninety-four.

Eight

Fate and Chance

Some people state confidently that Destiny rules all life. The source of that confidence is unknown.

It has been suggested by some human philosophers and scientists that although absolute laws apply to large units—such as all humanity or all atoms—an individual person, or a particular atom, may diverge in reacting to the law. Laws about a group of atoms can be formulated, physicist Werner Heisenberg discovered, but the exact location of a specific atom at a specific time cannot be ascertained.

Broad statements about the behavior of human beings can be made, but the conduct of each individual cannot be predicted. This fact has not kept fortune-tellers and astrologers from flourishing.

Roman emperor Marcus Aurelius repeatedly proclaimed the power of fate: "Whatever may happen to you, it was preordained for you from time everlasting." How Marcus knew so much about Destiny remains a mystery.

This is the same Marcus Aurelius who initiated the practice of throwing Christians to lions, an action that leads modern thinkers to question his judgment.

When men like Marcus Aurelius, and many others, assert that everyone's destiny has been pre-planned, they may find some difficulty in explaining why some human beings were born simply because a condom tore, or a dictator ordered women to bear more children, or a woman was raped. A planned design for the universe seems to have some flaws in the planning.

The French epigrammatist La Rochefoucauld rejected fatalism: "Although men flatter themselves with their great actions, they are not so often the result of great design as of chance."

Engineers, among many others, tend to be pessimistic when they cite Murphy's Law, "Everything that can go wrong will go wrong."

Some civilized human beings try to influence both chance and fate when they knock on wood to prevent bad luck.

William Bolitho made an interesting observation that all languages have made *fate* feminine.

English philosopher and mathematician Alfred North Whitehead thought that laws of nature are not necessarily permanent. They may change. Mutations and alterations of viruses support this idea.

Tibetans sometimes change their names after experiencing bad luck. Whether this is a successful maneuver is not certain.

Many people account for their failure by blaming it on destiny.

"When the gods want to punish us, they answer our prayers," many disappointed human beings have learned.

The most intriguing factor in human life seems to be chance. There are so many variables in life, so many unexpected and incalculable situations, that no one can accurately predict a person's future or guarantee the present. Diseases attack, economic conditions change, planes crash, fires erupt. Human beings benefit, and suffer, from an infinite number of possible occurrences. They like to quote from a Scottish poet, Robert Burns:

"The best laid schemes o' mice and men
Gang oft agley;
And lea'e us nought but grief and pain
For promis'd joy."

In our galaxy, the universe is indifferent to individual needs and desires. Human beings refuse to acknowledge this fact.

The precariousness of chance should make human beings humble. It rarely does.

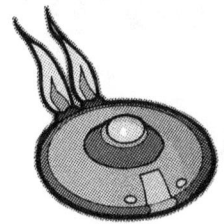

Nine

Aggression

There has always been so much conflict on Earth that one wonders whether conflict is the "normal" state of human society, and peace the artificial, temporary condition.

The veneer of civilization is very thin.

Human aggressiveness is expressed by some people in physical conflict and by others in violent defense of non-violence.

Aggression, by individuals and by nations, is always rationalized away with noble explanations.

Without hatred directed at a specific objective, some lives seem to have no meaning.

People resent one criticism more than they enjoy ten compliments.

An ancient Chinese proverb says: "It takes years to make a friend; it takes an hour to lose one."

In conflict, both individuals and groups always imitate the worst behavior of their opponents—never the best.

The weak, when they are in positions of power, are often more cruel than the strong.

It is not hard to prove, whoever your enemy is, that he is wicked.

When God gave Moses the commandment "Thou shalt not kill," he obviously didn't mean it. Often, in the Bible, God ordered Israel's rulers to kill men, women, and children of neighboring communities.

The universal interpretation of the Biblical commandment is: Thou shalt not kill, except when thou findest it convenient to kill.

Killing a great many people in other countries is the most likely way of being named a hero by historians.

All nations assume that their military victories prove the righteousness of their cause.

In the history of mankind only strength, or the illusion of strength, has protected mankind.

Every important nation is aggressive and acquisitive and deceptive.

Good behavior may be motivated more by fear of punishment than by genuine goodness.

If God did not want man to have guns He would not have permitted guns to be invented, contend some deep thinkers.

A question some people have asked is: Is it worse to commit violence spontaneously, as rioters do, or to commit violence after carefully fabricating justifications, as governments and courts do when they wage wars and support unjust legislation?

The person who hurts another—physically or psychologically—soon forgets the injury. The victim remembers, sometimes forever.

During World War Two the Nazi government of Germany sent novelist Erich Marie Remarque a bill to pay for their execution of his sister.

Professional hockey and basketball teams use "enforcers" whose primary task is to injure opposing athletes.

Some people feel that killing persons by rifles and swords is more objectionable than killing them by shelling and bombing. The views of victims have not been adequately solicited.

Vandalism, the destruction of something beautiful or venerable, has been practiced by human beings as long as there has been anything beautiful or venerable to destroy.

"You should forgive your enemies—but not until they've been hanged," said German poet Heinrich Heine.

American humorist Will Rogers quipped, "You can't say civilization doesn't advance, for in every war they kill you in a new way."

The Bible is quite aware of aggression, as the fifty-fifth Psalm shows: "I have seen violence and strife in the city . . . wickedness is in the midst thereof; deceit and guile depart not from the city's streets."

"Vengeance is mine," said the Lord, but a great many people have always volunteered to help Him.

There is no Society for the Prevention of Cruelty to Human Beings.

Ten

Deception

The more "civilized" a nation is, the more subtle are the deceptions that occur there.

Researchers have not determined whether the inclination to cheat is an inherited or acquired characteristic.

The more one learns about the actual operation of any institution, the more discrepancies one finds between the public image of that institution and the true condition prevailing.

To survive one must deceive, whether one is a human being or a tiny virus.

Nature practices deception with a cunning that the Italian politician Machiavelli might envy.

Forked tongues are not limited to white men.

The devil is not the only one who can quote out of context.

It is not seemly for rulers or executives to be aware of everything that is done on their behalf by subordinates.

Idealistic psychotherapists advise their patients, "Stop trying to seem what you are not." Few of their patients take their advice.

In India people were once hired to serve in claques, either applauding or making sounds of disapproval.

To avoid displaying an inappropriate reaction, many a would-be sophisticate trains himself or herself to show no reaction at all.

Lying is such a pervasive part of everyday existence that one psychologist calls it "a universal lubricant of social life."

Whenever a person begins a statement with the word "frankly," you can be sure that he or she is not being frank—and, presumably, that he or she has not been frank up to that point.

Even admirable qualities like politeness involve deception when the politeness is not sincere.

In a world full of evil, no one ever admits doing an evil thing.

Eleven

Hypocrisy

The more civilized a nation is, the more hypocritical it is.

The reason that "civilized" countries are the ones most permeated by hypocrisy is that they pretend to live by idealistic and noble principles. Since neither individuals nor institutions are capable of living up to these principles consistently, there is a greater gap between ideal and reality in the "advanced" countries than there is in the more "primitive" ones.

Subordination breeds hypocrisy. In a society where almost everyone is subordinate to someone else, almost everyone learns to behave hypocritically.

Group-hypocrisy is the same kind of casuistry by which an individual convinces himself, or herself, that what he or she is doing is wrong in general but right in this particular case.

A century ago the Italian scholar Vilfredo Pareto demonstrated that society rationalizes into dignity the defects of its institutions. Imitating the behavior of individuals, institutions always pretend that the reasons for their behavior are nobler than they really are.

Institutions, like individuals, almost never admit that their behavior is selfish or their philosophy self-serving. Institutions use the same devices for rationalizing that individuals use.

The military aggression of one's own country is nobly motivated; other nations are rapacious imperialists.

No nation has a monopoly on hypocrisy.

It is remarkable that in a world full of hypocrisy no one admits to being a hypocrite.

The chameleon is not a bad totem for some people.

The sentimentality of warriors and gangsters is quite selective.

A popular way for the wealthy to help the poor is to recite compassionate maxims.

People whose family members are accused of criminal behavior become very lenient in judging criminal behavior.

Merchants and businessmen do not apply the rules of their religion to their business practices.

In Italian poet Dante's *Divine Comedy*, hypocrites, in addition to enduring the expected inconveniences of Hell, are condemned to wear cloaks of lead.

The communist system in Soviet Russia took a perverse pleasure in pretending to give the masses precisely those freedoms that it denied them.

During the late unlamented experiment with a "classless" society the cruise-ships of Russia had four different classes of service. In Communist China a similar condition exists.

People adjust their behavior to different situations and practice in each situation the hypocrisy appropriate to it.

Historically, people have blamed their vicious actions on the commands of God; for noble behavior they take personal credit.

Rationalizing is the most universal psychological habit of human beings.

Young rebels ridicule the hypocrisies of the establishment, while they practice similar hypocrisies of their own.

According to the sacred writings of the Hebrew prophets: "Ten portions of wisdom, ten portions of law, and ten portions of hypocrisy are in the world."

Twelve

Gregariousness

Most human beings are gregarious creatures. But the inhabitants of the United States carry gregariousness to ridiculous extremes. More than a century ago French visitor Alexis de Tocqueville wrote, "Americans of all ages, all conditions, and all dispositions are forever forming associations." That tendency has continued and proliferated.

The *Encyclopedia of Associations* claims that 80% of Americans belong to organized groups. In addition to such conventional organizations as Rotarians, Kiwanians, Lions, Elks, Moose, (note the strange predilection for animal identification), Daughters of the American Revolution, neighborhood factions, educational associations, professional coalitions, and "political action committees," there are hundreds of groups to which a specialist, an aficionado, an admirer, or an eccentric can belong.

In the United States there are clubs interested in living creatures (elephants, miniature donkeys), non-living creatures (hobbits, vampires), collectibles (beer-bottle tops, sugar packets, glass dishes). There are also the American Association of Aardvark Aficionados, a National Chastity Society, and the Diving Dentists Society, among many, many others.

Symbols of membership in associations are very important to Americans. Many of them wear lapel pins to let the world know that they are proud members of Rotary (an international service club), or little gold keys to prove that they are Phi Beta Kappas (an elite intellectual organization), or some other object to indicate that they belong to a select group. These symbols are prized very highly.

These associations include "fan" clubs, groups of people who admire an entertainer or an athlete so much that they form an organization in his or her honor and celebrate the activities of their hero or heroine in various ways. Movie stars, popular singers, and outstanding athletes are the most frequent objects of such adoration, though they rarely get to meet any of their fatuous devotees. The life of a fan club is usually short, but new objects of mass adoration appear constantly.

Americans are famous for their hospitality, generously entertaining both friends and casual acquaintances. But American Benjamin Franklin wrote, "Fish and guests begin to smell after three days." And an old Chinese proverb says, "Few sights are as pleasant as the backs of departing guests."

Some people are gregarious because they genuinely enjoy the company of other people. Some are afraid of being alone. And some are so bored with themselves that they need the company of other bores.

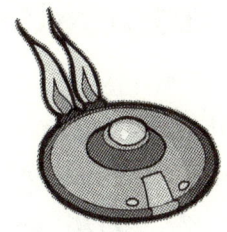

Thirteen

Conformity

In the lives of most human beings conformity is an enormously powerful force.

People don't ask "*Why* is this done?" but "*What* is done?" So a great many useless customs that no longer serve a practical purpose are maintained.

For many people the satisfaction with some of their pleasures and achievements stops being a satisfaction when someone whose opinion they value or fear denigrates those pleasures or achievements.

Gurdjieff wrote, "People worry too much about what other people think of them. They don't."

For some people what others think of them is more important than what they think of themselves.

Most people feel comfortable only with people like themselves, or people who pretend to be like them.

Conformity provides protection. That is why immigrants quickly change their names. Among human beings, as among other animals, being different can be very dangerous.

Many Americans buy and proudly wear caps and shirts that flaunt the names of professional sports teams or of universities that are successful in athletics. Idiocy is far more widely spread than IQ tests indicate.

Another example of fame-by-association consists of paying for the autographs of famous athletes.

Killing time in the proper manner is an important part of conformist existence.

Individuality in a conformist society is likely to be achieved only by a strong personality or an individual with a private income.

English mathematician S. H. Hardy wrote, "It is never worth a first-class man's time to express a majority opinion." But the outpouring of banalities continues unabated.

Fourteen

Deviation

Deviation among Earthlings consists of digression from the cultural norms and laws of one's own society.

What one society considers aberrant another society regards as normal.

Sociologist John Macionis writes, "Powerless people may be defined as deviant for exactly the same behavior that powerful people engage in with impunity."

Psychiatrist R. D. Laing suggests that insanity may be a perfectly rational adjustment in an insane world.

In every "civilized" society white-collar crime is treated more leniently than street crime, although the amounts of money lost to white-collar crimes are much greater.

Corporate crime is likely to be tried in a civil rather than a criminal court.

Society supports the punishment that its courts, at that time, happen to consider the proper punishment—with obvious exceptions for the rich, the powerful, and the beautiful.

One man's terrorist is another man's patriot.

God, the devil, the subconscious, the environment, and boredom have been blamed for human misbehavior. The person who commits the anti-social act usually considers himself, or herself, innocent or justified.

It is gross oversimplification to say that the cause of crime is economic need. The biggest crooks are rich men and women.

Crime is increasing everywhere in the world, except in small countries that whip graffiti-writers and cut off the hands of thieves.

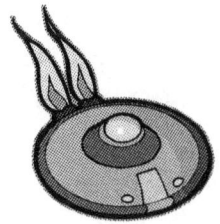

Fifteen

Human Peculiarities

It should not be surprising that the human animal behaves like an animal.

The human ego is so sensitive, so allergic to criticism, that it instantly fabricates justifications or excuses for its behavior.

Recent research suggests that the amount of happiness a person experiences may be genetically determined by the available levels of the brain chemical dopamine.

The person who confers a favor remembers it; the recipient of the favor quickly forgets.

Some people assume that the worst aspects of their personality are typical of everyone's secret self; that gives them consolation.

Naive liberals are almost as dangerous as naive reactionaries.

Some people who do not love any individuals convince themselves that they love all mankind.

Human beings are motivated by pleasure. Nothing—I am told—gives more pleasure than sex.

Human beings want to be loved for their own sakes, regardless of their achievements or failures.

When physical conflict occurs, intellectuals are likely to flee quickly.

Inconsistencies in logic have never prevented human beings from doing what they want to do.

People tend to treat as unimportant the things they can't do well—and exaggerate the significance of their skills.

People aware of their deficiencies often persuade themselves that good intentions are more important than brilliance.

For many human beings property, or status, becomes an extension of identity.

Few people who insist on the need to express themselves have much worth expressing.

When the average person looks inward, does he or she find much to see?

There is, at times, sheer joy in being alive—or so I am told.

Some sages claim that suffering ennobles—except when it embitters.

English poet A. E. Housman's lines apply to many human beings: "I, a stranger and afraid/ In a world I never made." But some humans share English poet W. S. Henley's delusion: "I am the master of my fate / I am the captain of my soul."

Englishman Oscar Wilde wrote, "I sometimes think that God, in creating man, somewhat overestimated his ability."

Sixteen

Culture

Some human anthropologists claim that there are five basic elements in every culture: symbols, language, norms, values, and materials.

It may be that *symbols* are a component of every culture. But everywhere symbols are interpreted, or misinterpreted, to suit the current need of the interpreter. For example, in light-skinned countries a light-colored skin has usually been considered preferable to a dark one. Even in dark-skinned Sri Lanka, in the fourth century, the Sigyria Frescoes showed Sinhalese noblewomen as light-colored and their attendants dark.

Language is defined as a system of symbols with standard meanings through which members of a society communicate with—and deceive—one another. The universal need to deceive is almost as important as the need to communicate. There are more than a thousand languages on Earth—and human beings try to mislead other human beings in every one of them. All languages in "civilized" countries have blatantly ambivalent meanings for words like honesty, loyalty, obligation, and compassion. And gossip is a prevailing element in all human conversations, the more revealing of someone else's misbehavior the better.

Norms are rules that prescribe, and proscribe, the behavior of members in a specific culture. Prescriptive norms order people to do certain things; consequently, people resent doing them. Proscriptive norms forbid people to do certain things—making those things immensely attractive.

The norms of one culture sometimes totally contradict the norms of another culture, but each group is convinced that its norms are the correct ones. Thus Americans are permitted to have only one legal wife at a time; Saudi Arabians are permitted four wives. Horses at stud are not limited to a specific number of contacts.

Values are standards by which members of a culture define what is desirable or undesirable, good or bad, beautiful or ugly. A belch is considered bad manners in the United States and a gracious tribute to the cook in China. Flatulence evokes an unfavorable reaction in both countries.

The *material* content of a culture consists of the physical objects made to satisfy the needs, desires, and whims of that culture. These products range from hand-made artifacts in primitive societies to complex electronic machines in advanced countries. There is an on-going controversy about the genuine value of advanced technology, in terms of its effect on human life. Cynics say there is no improvement in human nature. But optimists cite the indisputable advances in medical equipment, which save and prolong many lives. (In his book *Erewhon*, Samuel Butler prohibited the use of all inventions created after the Middle Ages. But that didn't improve things either.)

This lack of agreement among scholars should not disturb extraterrestrial visitors. It certainly does not disturb human scholars.

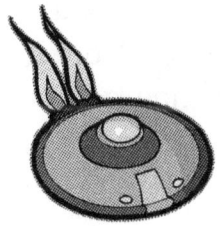

Seventeen

Social Organization

The enormous disparity between the image that each society on Earth projects for itself and the actual condition of that society is very amusing.

At extreme ends, social theorists who want to improve the world offer two approaches. If you create a good society, the individuals living in it will become good. Or, improve individuals, and they will create a good society. Neither condition has been quite attained yet. Not all individuals are good nor has a user-friendly society yet been concocted.

A Viennese eccentric named Sigmund Freud wrote, "Civilization is repression."

Society rewards what it really needs—doctors, protectors, influence peddlers—and what it really wants—entertainers, courtesans, athletes. Society does not adequately reward those people whom idealists assume society should reward, such as clergy, teachers, and nurses.

Most human beings do not like to live alone and apparently never have. "Social life," says historian Arnold Toynbee, "is older than the human race itself; it is found among insects and animals."

Christianity and competition seem incompatible—but Western society is based on both cooperation and contention.

As long as membership in certain groups is restricted, entrance into those groups is going to seem desirable to some people.

Social climbers have no sense of humor.

Being in the upper class of a society does not guarantee that one becomes a well-adjusted or happy human being.

Sigmund Freud said that people in groups revert to an infantile state. His daughter Anna believed that defense mechanisms are "shared by individuals and families as well as larger units." And Robert Boles concluded that members of a group have the same fantasy life.

To a semiotician everything in society, from the patterns on the wallpaper to the inanity of popular television programs, is a clue to the real meaning of phenomena. Unfortunately semioticians do not agree on precisely what these real meanings are.

Chauvinism is the conviction of one group that it is superior to all other groups, as among males, fundamentalists, and Frenchmen.

In advanced civilizations individual humans know more and more but can do less and less about what they know.

The closer to the truth unpleasant remarks are, the more furious the establishment becomes—at the maker of the remarks.

If the only time people are willing to cooperate and sacrifice is during emergencies, like war, perhaps the ideal social climate is a permanent emergency.

The twentieth century, the century of the greatest technological progress, was also the century of heinous brutality.

Ants are the only non-humans who wage wars for plunder, commit atrocities after their battles, have a strong sense of property, and keep other insects as slaves.

The most appropriate comment on human society may be that of entomologist William Morton Wheeler, a profound student of the social life of insects. He showed that insects also can maintain complex communities without the use of reason.

Eighteen

Stratification

In every human society different levels of status are assigned to every individual.

Asians are well aware of this. In Sri Lanka there is a saying: "It is good to be a Headman, even in Hell." And the Japanese have a proverb: "Betters have their betters; inferiors have their inferiors."

Old money usually gets more respect than new money.

Equality is a fine thing in principle, but there are limits to the application of uncomfortable principles in the U.S.A.

In every society there is considerable antipathy on the part of lower-level people towards those above them. This antipathy tends to dissipate when individuals achieve a higher status.

A 1991 survey published as *Day of Truth* asked Americans to rank occupations they most admired. Among the top twenty were scientists, college professors, clergy, airline pilots, paramedics, firemen, and farmers. At the bottom of the list were lawyers, car salesmen, Congressmen, prostitutes, TV evangelists, organized crime bosses, and drug dealers.

Animals that live in groups abide by a rigid hierarchy in which each animal knows what his or her position is and behaves accordingly. Except when ambition or resentment makes the animal rebel against the existing hierarchy.

When female barn swallows cheat on their mates, they always copulate with males who have longer tails than their mates. And female chickadees whose mates are low in the hierarchy conduct all their adulterous affairs with higher-ranked males. Human beings have no monopoly on social climbing.

Nineteen

American Society

The basic, fundamental, inescapable characteristic of American society is the need for money. It determines one's security, one's quality of life, one's associates. The moment one's money is gone, everything collapses. One's housing changes, one's food changes, one's friends change. It is impolite to mention, but money is the predominant element in American life.

Money does not guarantee happiness, but it makes unhappiness easier to bear.

As the Bible says, "To accumulate riches in order to indulge in luxury is not in accord with God's will." No American believes this.

A sociologist who analyzed the most common values of American society lists equal opportunity first and racial prejudice tenth. There seems to be some contradiction here, but both values exist in the U.S.A.

Americans are not born holding telephones to their ears, although that may be the impression a visitor gets.

Almost all American adults wear wristwatches—men to keep appointments and women to be fashionably late.

Americans treat white-clad persons with respect even when they are on television.

The love of money is not limited to Americans. A Sri Lankan proverb states, "Seeing Money's power, Respectability went slinking to hide itself in the thicket."

The U.S has created a high standard of living—which is very pleasant, for those who can afford a high standard of living.

In the United States, especially during the nineteenth century, more than a hundred communities tried to establish Utopian societies. None of them survived.

The time for anyone to be Number One in the United States is short.

American essayist Henry David Thoreau wrote, "The mass of men lead lives of quiet desperation." In modern America the sounds of desperation are terribly noisy.

What makes the United States the most desirable country in the world for immigrants is the idea of freedom. But freedom is a two-edged sword. Everyone has the right to start his or her own business—but nine out of ten businesses fail within five years. Everyone is free to become a farmer—but the number of farms diminishes every year. Everyone can seek whatever job he or she wants—but the number of desirable jobs is limited.

This freedom gives people the opportunity to succeed and the chance to fail. Human beings seem more pleased by the former than they are by the latter.

There are a few small grounds for discontent in the U.S.A. A number of citizens seem disturbed by the crumbling cities where no one is safe at night, the polluted air, the contaminated water, the uncontrolled erosion of the soil, and the overpopulation encouraged by different groups for different but always selfish reasons.

All of this deterioration has no similarity at all to the decline of the Roman Empire, American historians insist.

Twenty

Family

In the United States the nuclear family typically consists of two parents and their children. The extended family, in less industrialized societies, includes parents, children, and other kin such as grandparents, aunts, uncles, and cousins. The nuclear family accepts fewer responsibilities for these relatives than does the extended family. But the members of nuclear families manage to exploit all the useful connections that an extended family provides.

The typical middle-class family among white Americans comprises two parents, 1.6 children, and a psychotherapist.

No marriage can survive the constant expression of uncomfortable truths.

The inability to find a new spouse is sometimes disguised as loyalty to the old one.

I am told that the successful husband-wife relationship is based on compromise. But I have observed that the compromising varies from fifty/fifty to ninety-five/five, favoring either the female or the male.

Like all other human institutions, marriage has elicited some cynical comments. Honoré de Balzac, a French novelist, wrote, "Most husbands remind me of an orangutan trying to play the violin."

English social scientist Herbert Spencer defined marriage as "a ceremony in which rings are put on the finger of the lady and through the nose of the gentleman."

An ancient Ceylonese saying shows that in Asia, too, family relationships were not always perfect: "Six months after the death of the mother-in-law a tear came into the eye of the daughter-in-law."

Contradictions in theories about child-care are flagrant, persistent, and amusing. Fortunately, most children survive whatever theory is current at the time their parents bring them up.

The love-versus-discipline conflict goes back a long way. "Spare the rod and spoil the child" is a very old proverb. But twentieth-century psychology recommends affection instead of punishment.

A few unsolved problems remain. Should one ever punish children? Does indiscriminate love breed security or spoiling? Does discipline make children mature or bitter? Are all child abusers people who were physically punished when they were children? (Recent statistics reveal much more child abuse than was previously assumed.)

There are additional uncertainties. Do strict parents or lenient parents produce happier children? More successful children? Some experts disparage a democratic, indulgent structure in a family. Other experts blame authoritarian parents for the subsequent problems of their children. Should the father be stern, the mother forgiving? But that procedure results in dislike of the father. Reverse? That does not always work either. Fortunately, parents ignorant of contemporary educational theory often manage to turn out decent and healthy children.

Although Confucianism is credited with building a solid family structure in China, it is China that produced such cynical proverbs as, "Children do not go mad worrying about their parents," and "There are few loving children at the bedsides of long-sick parents." Upper and lower class families in the U.S. have more children than the middle class—the rich because they can afford them, and the lower classes because they marry earlier and use birth control less.

Studies show that infants who had not been caressed become obstreperous several months earlier than those who had been fondled often.

The rebellious behavior of children is described by psychologists as the normal development of individual personalities.

In the animal kingdom there is little monogamy. More than thirty percent of the baby birds in any nest were sired by a different bird than the male who is helping to feed them.

Furthermore, research by ethnologists rejects long-held beliefs about fidelity among animal couples. As American journalist Natalie Augin puts it, "Two cygnet swans remain coupled for life . . . with just a bit of adultery, cuckoldry, and gang rape on the side."

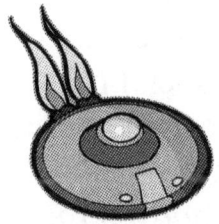

Twenty-one

Pretense

Pretense is an indispensable element of life in human society. The more "civilized" a society is, the more numerous are the examples of dissimulation.

People wear invisible masks in public. (In Eugene O'Neill's play *Great God Brown* the characters actually put on different masks when they assume different social roles.)

In a book he calls *By the Grace of Guile*, philosopher Loyal Rue admits that the universe is indifferent to individual human needs and desires. But most Earthlings find this fact unbearable. It interferes with personal happiness and social coherence. So human beings have concocted myths, lies, and illusions to create a more pleasant ambience for existence. Rue assumes that the universal myths, including concepts of God, are grand fictions, but he insists that without such lies humanity cannot survive.

In the United States, hospitals do not dun, they seek "reimbursement." A patient who dies suffers "negative patient-care outcome." Wiretaps are "technical collection sources." An October crash in the stock market was described as a "fourth-quarter equity retreat." The Chrysler Motor Company's layoff of 5,000 workers was really "a career alternative enhancement program." And, in the U.S. Navy, high waves have been officially described as "climatic disturbances at the air-sea interface."

Also, a Canadian mayor called a radioactive waste-dump "a containment initiative." An activist group in Canada proposed that news media substitute for "prostitute" the term "sex industry workers." And in the mid-1990s Panama invasion, the U.S. Army described civilian casualties as "collateral damage."

In a number of columns he called "Antics with Semantics," Sydney J. Harris showed how language is used to distort the truth in daily life. For example: I am "flexible"; you are "malleable"; he is "just putty." I "couldn't pass up the opportunity"; you "couldn't resist the temptation"; he "couldn't turn down a fast buck." My plan is a "strategy"; your plan is a "scheme"; his plan is a "dodge."

In a book called *Double Speak* William Lutz lists a number of current American euphemisms: A discharged person is not fired but dehired, non-retained, non-renewed, selected out. Or, the company undergoes head-count reduction, negative employment retention, restructuring, or downsizing.

Smog becomes "a slight imperfection of the atmosphere." And garage mechanics are now "service advisers." Janitors are "sanitary engineers." A bodyguard is a "protection specialist." And spies have become "intelligence specialists."

The British Museum's recent exhibit of 3,000 years of the forger's art included the following. Priests in ancient Babylon faked an inscription to make their temple seem a thousand years older than it really was. "The objects in the exhibit range from a faked Roman chariot and photographs of fairies to a forged Rembrandt painting and a witch's wreath . . . fake jewels, coins, sculptures, fossils, furniture and porcelain. There's even a letter purporting to be written by Jesus Christ." A Scottish museum faked a fish with fur to satisfy public demand.

In a suburb of Toronto a real-estate developer uses actors and models to play the roles of happy homeowners while he shows prospective purchasers through the premises. The actors move through rooms, play cards, and bake cookies as they create an atmosphere of casual geniality.

Also, Actors Guild members in the United States are hired to play the roles of relatives at sparsely attended weddings and of guests at parties whose hosts want to create the impression of popularity. And the people who laugh on laugh tracks of unamusing television comedies are not really engaging in spontaneous merriment.

Some pretenses seem harmless. Ann Landers is not really Ann Landers, Dear Abby is not Abby, and Betty Crocker is not Betty Crocker. Nor do attractive dogs and charmingly stout cats really endorse canine and feline products.

Pretense is so pervasive in American society that it is accepted as a necessary element of civilized existence.

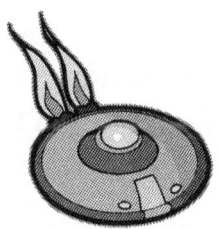

Twenty-two

Ritual

Such rituals as baptism are intended to improve the infant's chances in this world and the next. There's no way of knowing if this is effective.

Social organizations such as Elks, Masons, fraternities, and many others have secret passwords and rites that they are forbidden to disclose to non-members. At the funerals of their members the Masons wear ridiculous clothes and perform certain rituals. The Shriners put on silly hats and indulge in public high jinks. For some reason, this juvenile behavior provides great satisfaction to the participants.

When white American males shake hands they try to give a strong, firm handshake, with direct eye contact. This is supposed to demonstrate mutual respect, equality of status, strength, and sincerity. But the handshake of a Navaho Indian serves a very different ritualistic purpose. The Navaho does not look the other person in the eye, for that may indicate anger or irritation. Instead, he holds the hand gently, so as not to disturb the natural flow of feeling between his own state of being and the feelings of the other person.

Important officials are sworn into their new jobs in a public ceremony where they put their hands on a Bible and swear to do their duty honestly, so help them God. Whether God is ever aware of his obligation is doubtful, but the officials never violate this pledge. Of course.

For many parents a daughter's wedding constitutes a challenge to display their wealth—or to display wealth they pretend they have.

Most of the participants in a "proper" American wedding don't know why many of the wedding rituals are performed—and couldn't care less.

Romans thought—mistakenly—that an artery ran from the third finger to the heart, making that finger an appropriate place for a wedding ring.

The number of virgin brides wearing white in modern American weddings has diminished considerably.

Neither the brides who promise to obey the groom, nor the brides who omit the promise, pay the slightest attention to it after they are married.

Some American divorces are celebrated with parties similar to the wedding festivity.

In the United States when one meets a casual acquaintance and says, "How are you?" one should expect to be answered "Fine," even when the acquaintance has a terminal illness.

On April Fool's Day people play many practical jokes, revealing how much pleasure they get out of humiliating others.

Many American holidays are used by merchants to sell gifts. Mother's Day was originally created by florists, and Father's Day became a natural excuse to sell everything—allowing children a month between the two holidays to save some money for gifts.

When a catastrophe occurs a high public official appears at the spot, makes a cursory inspection, and announces over television that the tragedy is in the hearts and prayers of the administration. This provides enormous relief to the victims.

The ritualized response to the rising crime rate involves a pledge by a government official to make more severe laws, expand capital punishment, and build more prisons. The fact that none of these procedures works is irrelevant.

In Asia the color white is associated with funerals, whereas black is used in the West.

Most rituals are carry-overs from an earlier period, customs that are now silly rather than awesome. But some rituals, such as funerals and memorials, serve a therapeutic purpose by providing closure to distressing events.

Most rituals are obsolete. But since people don't know that these rituals are obsolete, they continue to observe them just as if they still made sense. To the uninvolved extraterrestrial visitor, it's a very funny world.

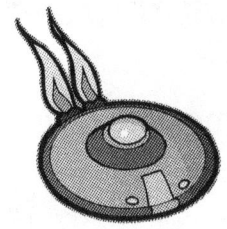

Twenty-three

Government

Politics, like most human activities, is based on expediency.

A person can take any political position, ranging from extreme radicalism to extreme conservatism, and later find an eminent philosopher who supports it.

Although powerful nations consider it impolite to say that might makes right, there is a strong suspicion prevailing that such is the case.

Trust among thieves and politicians is not absolute.

Niccolo Machiavelli was an Italian political theorist whose cynical pragmatism is condemned by everyone and practiced by everyone.

Brutal behavior by nations and institutions is aided by the fact that nations and institutions have no guilty consciences.

All twentieth-century genocides have been whitewashed by the groups that committed them, and by the nations that permitted them to be committed.

Politicians often abstain from exposing the sins of other politicians to prevent them from exposing their own sins. Everyone has a skeleton in the closet—or, at least, some bones.

One of the distasteful things about being a liberal is the necessity to pretend a liking for obnoxious liberals. Conservatives have a similar problem with obnoxious conservatives.

Americans celebrate a Fool's day every other November. They call it Election Day.

It is to spread God's word, or to bring civilization to barbarians, or to free downtrodden masses that strong nations invade weak ones—never because they are trying to extend their economic interests or their political power.

Many people consider the title "United Nations" an oxymoron.

In politics, you have to expect a certain amount of corruption. The rule is: take according to rank.

Freedom is the opportunity to do what one wants to do, as long as one does only the things the government permits one to do.

In free societies the amount of liberty the public enjoys varies greatly, but it is always less than what people think they have.

The Soviet Union was a communist aberration based on Karl Marx's failure to admit that other human beings had the same faults as he had.

A neoconservative is a former liberal who is now as certain of the virtues of conservatism as he or she was once certain of the virtues of liberalism.

Totalitarianism is a system of open repression by the government, as distinguished from political systems that repress indirectly.

Democrats and Republicans take turns in mismanaging the U.S.A.

Republicans are more conservative than Democrats, preferring traditional blundering to faulty attempts at change.

Republicans and Democrats take turns at failing to keep campaign promises.

In politics there are no permanent friends or enemies.

No political action committee is motivated by altruism.

Everyone who is working for a cause is also working for himself or herself.

A distaste for power is considered a weakness; excessive ambition is criticized only when it fails.

When rulers choose which painful alternatives to follow, it is the masses who suffer the pain.

Many underdeveloped countries fail to realize that what is good for their benefactors (i.e., the developed countries) is not necessarily good for them.

The rich are much more skillful in avoiding taxes than are the poor.

It is safer to be feared than to be loved. (Machiavelli is not the only one who realized this.)

It is hard to believe that the modern Congress is quite what the Founding Fathers visualized for the future.

A synonym for "deception" is "diplomacy."

American satirist H. L. Mencken wrote: "only a country that is rich and safe can afford to be a democracy."

Everyone knows, but no one admits, that treaties last only until it is expedient to break them.

There is not much room for an honest man in politics.

"Power corrupts"—almost as much as lack of power corrupts.

The United States is not a "melting pot" but a stew of incompatible ingredients.

No political system can please everybody.

Twenty-four

Bureaucracy

Administrators, having once been human, sometimes retain a few decent qualities that hinder them in their administrative careers.

The successful administrator soon discards all pretense to compassion, honesty, and unambiguous speech.

Being a whistle-blower, in private industry or in the government, is not an enviable activity. One complainant put it this way: "If you have God, the law, the press, and the facts on your side, you have a 50/50 chance of winning."

Many bureaucrats work under a severe handicap: They are stupid.

Bureaucracies have evolved to make government function—and to slow up its functioning.

One of the characteristics of bureaucracy is to make decent bureaucrats behave as badly as sadistic ones.

"Treat with extreme prejudice" is a military euphemism for "kill." It is a perfect example of bureaucratic language.

The logistics of an institution often interfere with the ideals of the institution.

Twenty-five

Law

Sometimes laws that are reasonable in theory prove to be absurd in individual cases. People who use "excessive force" in defending their property are made to pay enormous sums to the unsuccessful criminals.

Lawyers are paid large sums for proving that guilty clients are innocent. This is not quite what the Founding Fathers intended when they postulated that a person is presumed to be innocent until proved guilty.

Good lawyers get for their clients better results than do poor lawyers. Justice is very flexible.

In the Middle Ages a Persian definition of a lawyer was, "a person who is willing to tell any lie."

Stealing by legal means is not called stealing.

Certain law magazines carry ads for experts who are willing to testify on every conceivable subject. This is, of course, a more sophisticated procedure than choosing lying witnesses from the volunteering crowds who waited outside the courts of ancient Athens.

Juries make their decisions not on the basis of facts but on two irrelevant factors: their own prejudices and the skills of the opposing lawyers.

Recently a speaker at a law school graduation said, "You now have a license to steal."

The judge always believes the person who says he or she is guilty. The judge never believes the person who claims innocence.

French critic Anatole France wrote, "The law, in its majestic equality, forbids the rich as well as the poor to sleep under bridges, to beg in the streets, and to steal bread."

It is said that once in an American court a man jumped up and cried, "Judge, I demand justice." The judge looked at him in surprise and said, "What have I to do with justice? This is a court of law."

Twenty-six

Business

Businessmen approve the laissez-faire economic theories of Adam Smith, except when help by the government proves more useful to business than laissez-faire economics.

Although they vociferously proclaim their patriotism, many large American manufacturers have moved their factories into countries that pay much lower wages to workers.

Supply-side economic theory implies that making the rich richer on Earth will make the poor richer in heaven.

A labor union is an organization dedicated to the welfare of laborers and of the officers of labor unions.

Salaries in the U.S. have no relationship to the moral, social, or humanitarian value of the service rendered.

While a priest may earn $5 an hour, a plumber in Colorado earns $75. A trip to heaven is a distant possibility; a stuffed toilet is an immediate problem.

The altruism of corporate business is exceeded only by its greed, its ruthlessness, and its hypocrisy.

Insurance companies dedicate themselves to maximizing premium and minimizing payments.

Mafiosos are avowed criminals, as distinguished from corporations and stock-market manipulators.

Businessmen rarely stop handling a sales item simply because it is harmful.

The American stock market goes down when it hears good news (such as full employment) and up when it hears bad news (a powerful nation threatening to attack a small country).

In the U.S. today, after thirty days' use a luxury becomes a necessity.

Although a Jewish proverb says, "Shrouds have no pockets," most people try to fill their pockets while they are alive.

In the final analysis, the definitive criterion in business is the bottom line and only the bottom line.

In business there is only one law: survival of the fittest. That fitness has nothing to do with morality or compassion or decency.

Business is one aspect of civilization in which Social Darwinism (survival of the fittest) functions, totally and ruthlessly.

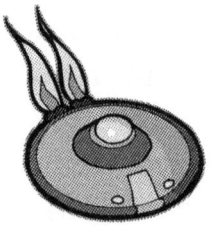

Twenty-seven

Advertising

Two centuries ago British poet Samuel Coleridge wrote that to appreciate literature one needs "a willing suspension of disbelief." The American public has enthusiastically adopted that attitude toward advertising.

Human beings prefer pleasant fictions to unpleasant truths. Advertising thrives on this condition.

Slogans persuade more successfully than elaborate arguments because most people are "cognitive misers," always trying to conserve mental energy and attention.

Although many of the advertisements in the United States are insults to the average intelligence, they sell the products they advertise.

Women are shown to be psychotic about cleanliness; they walk around their houses smelling the rugs, the kitchen, the bathroom, the newly washed clothing. And they express ecstatic delight when informed that a miraculous product is available to provide perfect cleanliness and an atmosphere that other women will envy.

Men are offered regrowth of hair, larger muscles, and youthfulness, almost instantaneously. And ads for the two most widely used drugs in America—liquor and cigarettes—unceasingly provide images of handsome, happy, popular individuals who are drinking or smoking.

Stephen Leacock, a humorist trained in economics, wrote: "Advertising may be described as the science of arresting human intelligence long enough to get money from it." H. G. Wells was more scathing: Advertising, he said, is legalized lying.

Twenty-eight

Science

Because scientists use a jargon that other human beings don't understand, most of their disputes remain concealed from the public.

Every day human beings obtain new scientific information, some of it modifying or contradicting what was previously thought to be true.

In his study of the time-lag between a discovery in science and the acceptance of that discovery by the scientific community, American professor Thomas Kuhn found that five to ten years pass before older scientists stop ridiculing or ignoring the new information, which makes obsolete their previous assumptions.

Some "scientists" still accept the notion that the Earth, with all its trimmings, was created by God in one busy six-day period.

Proponents of the Chaos theory suggest that universal laws of nature create order out of apparent disorder. And nobody knows what killed off the dinosaurs.

The "black holes" in outer space have not been commercialized yet, but it is only a matter of time until the advertising appears.

An eminent English astronomer, John Hawley, offers an alternative theory to Darwin's evolution: A Visiting Cosmic Intelligence started the human species on Earth.

On my galaxy all activity originates in tension between apparent opposites. It seems to me that this may also be true on Earth. Even atoms are positive or negative, and the presence of both charges is necessary to produce action.

Even in a totally computerized world no one will have complete understanding, as the early users of computers admitted when they coined the aphorism, "Garbage in, garbage out."

Computers cannot solve social problems or answer questions about God, love, happiness, and the purpose of human existence. Perhaps it's just as well.

Twenty-nine

Technology

The new technology and new electronics permit human beings to achieve more quickly the same objectives that they achieved more slowly before.

Modern technology provides instant revelation of the world's social problems, but it does nothing to help solve these problems.

Technology, like the laws of nature, is amoral.

Henry David Thoreau wrote, "Inventions are likely to be improved means to unimproved ends."

Thirty

Medicine

One must give medicine credit for the enormous advances it made during the twentieth century. Medications have been created or discovered which cure previously fatal diseases, as well as healing a great many illnesses that were once untreatable. Surgical techniques have been developed which almost miraculously save lives that only a few years ago would have been lost.

Like other professionals, doctors disagree over many medical procedures. A "second opinion" often contradicts the first.

American doctors discourage people from getting ill on weekends, since treating patients interferes with the doctors' recreation. And in ancient China this proverb was coined: "The doctor who rides in a chair will not visit the house of the poor."

Also in ancient China an interesting custom existed. Doctors were paid exorbitant amounts to cure serious illnesses—but if the royal patient died, the doctor could be sent to prison or executed. I don't know whether this custom resulted in more patients and doctors living longer, but I presume it did.

There is no denying that medicine has made enormous progress in recent years. Comparable advances have been made in military devices, especially of the nuclear variety. Two of the greatest achievements of the twentieth century were in weaponry and in medicine.

Human beings can now kill better and heal better than at any time in the past.

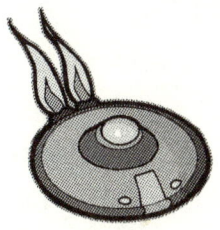

Thirty-one

Health

A study by the Brookings Institute suggests that preventive medicine may be more expensive than treating sick patients.

Studies of health habits have proliferated—and many of them contradict each other. One study concluded that people who use conventional blankets live longer than those who use electric blankets. A great many apparently innocuous foods and objects have been accused of being dangerous to one's health. A recent study at the University of California, San Francisco, reported that omitting fat from one's diet increased the life-span by only three or four months. Drinking coffee has proved to be harmful, or harmless. And left-handed people die nine years earlier than right-handers, two psychologists report; other studies claim that the shortfall for lefties is only two years.

Similarly, a worldwide review of cholesterol in 1992 challenged long-accepted beliefs. The new evidence indicates that, among women, cholesterol levels appeared to have no influence on how often they died from other causes. And, among men, the only groups who died more often were those whose cholesterol was either very high or very low.

Linus Pauling won two Nobel Prizes for engaging in two impossible missions: stopping wars and curing the common cold.

In the Middle Ages the Devil was blamed for most mental illnesses. Today the explanations vary from childhood traumas to chemical imbalance.

Recent discoveries in neurobiology indicate that many mental illnesses may be biological or genetic, not the result of bad parenting or willful idiosyncrasy.

Studies show that low-calorie diets combined with behavior modification are only 10% successful.

From the point of view of American nutritionists the French eat all the wrong foods, wrongly prepared. But they have less trouble with clogged arteries and cholesterol than Americans. Regular temperate drinking of wine may be the French secret of good health.

AIDS has been called the Black Plague of modern civilization, and some religious fanatics claim that it is God's way of punishing the wicked. Surprisingly, some religious fanatics have died of AIDS.

Two simple solutions to human medical problems have been offered. Nancy Reagan suggested, "Just say no to drugs." According to American satirist Mark Russell, the planners of the Republican Party health plan said, "Just say no to sickness." I can't understand why these solutions were not immediately adopted.

Albert Schweitzer, a famous humanitarian, said happiness is good health and a bad memory.

Thirty-two

Education

There is no consensus in the United States on whether the purpose of education should be utilitarian or humanistic, specific or general, intensive or gradual.

American students choose curricula not for intellectual growth but for help in finding desirable employment. Subsistence always takes precedence over "culture."

It is the unmeasurable components of a general education that enrich the remaining lives of university graduates. That counts for nothing with prospective employers.

Learning and pain have a common evolutionary origin. The brain uses similar biochemical procedures for learning and for minimizing damage after an injury.

The United States is a "credential" society, meaning that a person needs an advanced degree before he or she can be employed in some occupations. I have noted, however, that there is often little connection between the credential and competency.

Scholars tend to be as dogmatic as everyone else. A retiring president of a large university listed the ingredients for a successful program: "Provide football for the alumni, sex for the students, and parking for the faculty."

Public meetings conducted by university administrators are likely to consist of articulate duplicity.

Students at prestigious universities suffer because these institutions value research above teaching skill.

Some university presidents are required by contract to receive a smaller salary than the coach of the football team.

Many educators who are incompetent in teaching and research become incompetent, but better paid, administrators.

When average Americans are made aware of their ignorance of history and philosophy, they seem proud of it.

Many scholars are inclined to tell people a lot more than they want to know.

At American universities amateur scholar-athletes are neither amateurs nor scholars.

Ambrose Bierce defined an "American academy" as "A modern school where football is taught."

Universities dismiss character-building coaches whose teams lose games. The same universities then hire corrupt coaches whose teams do win games. No hypocrisy is ever admitted in the process.

Aldous Huxley thought the educated and uneducated share the same beliefs and prejudices, but the former are more articulate in expressing these beliefs and prejudices.

Bertrand Russell, an educator as well as a philosopher, wrote: "Some children are born with the ability to think; our schools are designed to cure them of this habit."

The hatred of religious and ethnic groups has to be taught. No one is born hating Jews, Muslims, Blacks, or Croatians. That kind of education has been successful all over the world.

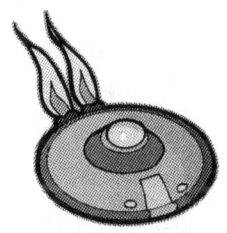

Thirty-three

Entertainment

Since the inhabitants of our galaxy do not waste energy on any unproductive activities it is difficult to explain the word "entertainment" to an extraterrestrial visitor. But human beings spend so much time in this activity that I must try to describe it.

Human need—or assumed need—for entertainment begins in infancy. Almost every society provides toys for its infants and children to play with. And adults exhibit the most ludicrous behavior with babies, playing peek-a-boo, uttering silly sounds like koochie-koo, and making asinine faces in the effort to entertain a child.

As soon as human beings rise above the level of subsistence they begin looking for means of entertaining themselves. They are remarkably ingenious in creating activities that provide, or simulate, play. Whether it is escape from boredom or a search for controlled competition that motivates people is not clear.

Americans seem to have an irresistible desire to fill every free moment with some activity or emotion. There is widespread fascination with pornography. Mood changes are provided by drugs and alcohol. And there has been an enormous expansion in the number of electronic games and the availability of take-home movies and videos. Few Americans seem to find life itself stimulating enough to be satisfying. Of course, many other animals also enjoy playing, so perhaps it's not so surprising.

Boredom may explain why dangerous activities fascinate many people. High rides at carnivals, parachute-jumping, mountain-climbing, bungee-jumping—all provide Earthlings the chance of sudden death.

Men and women who perform perilous feats or experience hazardous adventures provide vicarious excitement for more timid human beings. And writers and filmmakers who concoct exciting conflicts, pitting human beings against one another, or against nature, find an enormous audience for their products. Repressed aggression, in little old ladies as well as rambunctious children, is apparent everywhere.

Americans are not alone in seeking danger. In Japan people take pride in eating puffer-fish, a delicacy which, when imperfectly prepared, causes instant death. In Spain there is a city, Pamplona, where once a year bulls are permitted to run through the crowded streets while Earthlings try to avoid being trampled. And there is always Russian roulette, which is not limited to Russia. (In Russian roulette a handgun filled with five blanks and one bullet is held to one's temple and fired.)

Still another universal form of compensating for boredom is gambling. Gambling is the risking of money or other valuable things on the outcome of something involving chance or competition. It is an obsession indulged in by some people all the time and most people some of the time.

Card games are popular all over the world. The game called bridge, for example, provides entertainment for millions. Housewives meet in friends' homes to play, while more addicted players attend bridge clubs regularly and take bridge cruises to different ports without ever getting off the ship. Newspapers run columns of advice on playing bridge most effectively; players count the points they win in the effort to become Life Masters; and divorces take place over differences of opinion as to how certain hands should have been played. For many

Americans, bridge provides the most interesting activity of their lives.

An enormous amount of time is spent by Americans in reading fiction. Some of these imaginary tales are insightful, profound, and illuminating. But the vast majority consists of stories concocted by formula to satisfy the fantasies of a discontented public. Adventure is provided vicariously by Western and espionage fiction.

Some basic human need is apparently satisfied by detective stories in which murders are committed and the perpetrators are always caught. These vary from genteel killings in English villages to serial murders in brutal urban locales. Westerns, detective stories, and suspense fiction have been called adult fairy tales. They exist because there is a huge demand for them.

This in spite of the fact that 45% of Americans never read books.

The readers of light fiction are often also devotees of long running soap operas on television. These are so popular that viewers send gifts to the fictional characters, mourn their fabricated deaths, and subscribe to magazines which keep them up to date on the activities in the soap operas. I know that a visitor from another galaxy will find it hard to believe that civilized human beings engage in such actions, but all I can do is report facts as they exist.

American radio is non-judgmental, transmitting the most absurd and vicious statements with the same conviction as wise and useful remarks.

Something called "music" is not only enormously popular but almost a necessity for Americans. Technically, it is the art of combining tones into a composition having structure and continuity, rhythm, melody, or harmony. At its best, music can create intensely moving, sometimes spiritual effects.

But for some people music becomes addictive. They turn on the radio or a compact disc or a cassette the moment they awake. When they go out they put on a device over both ears that provides music while they travel. And many people living alone feel a compulsion to have some form of music playing all the time.

One of the characteristics of vocal music is that it can make the most trivial statements seem important and the most shallow cliches seem profound. Both opera and "rap" music share this dubious distinction.

The late Jerry Garcia, a popular rock-music guitarist, said that his band, The Grateful Dead, provided its fans with "a tear in reality"—a brief escape from the mundane.

When something is too silly to be spoken, sing it, said H. L. Mencken.

Chevrolet advertises that one of its new models is made by the country that invented rock and roll. This is intended to be a recommendation, not an apology.

Another very popular activity is dancing. It consists of a series of gyrations in prescribed form to the accompaniment of music. In America millions of people love to dance, some in formal ballrooms. Others enjoy ethnic, folk, and "country" dancing, jumping around in energetic and unusual routines.

For men the most popular diversions seem to be golf, bowling, and copulating.

Another form of pleasure for human beings is collecting. Wealthy people collect masterpieces of art, or what "experts" tell them are masterpieces of art. People with limited incomes collect an incredible variety of objects, ranging from the useful and potentially valuable to totally useless and valueless. In the latter category are old wire and cheap chinaware.

An eminent psychoanalyst, Otto Rank, wrote that the turn to religion, art, or collecting is an unconscious search for permanent things in a world of constant change.

The synthetic creation of art is not the only defect of American entertainment. A recent survey indicates that a majority wants a large amount of violent action and steamy sex in their entertainment.

Humor is a very popular element in American entertainment. It appears in the form of jokes, witticisms, and epigrams. Plays, novels, and television comedies utilize humor. So it is worth explaining how humor works.

The psychology of humor, on Earth, is playful aggression. The technique of humor is unexpected distortion of familiar material. All humor is directed at somebody or something. This is as true in my galaxy as it is on Earth.

All of these characteristics of popular entertainment in the United States combine to create an atmosphere of prodigious banality, cheapness, and insensitivity. American television, movies, and radio provide dishonest ads, squealing laughter, obscene invasion of privacy, and a marketplace for the expression of every conceivable idiocy.

My host says that modern television has lost all the traditional concepts of good taste, decency, and morality that once characterized American values. The same trend, I am told, also dominates modern literature, and the scenes now depicted, as well as the language used, were in the past limited to the gutter and the private quarters of perverts.

Americans who died before World War Two were very fortunate in that they never had to listen to rock-and-roll music, pay attention to idiotic talk-shows on radio, or look at TV shows in which people confess their private, and often contemptible, behaviors.

In what is capriciously called "civilized" society, human development has advanced from seeking the basic necessities for survival to contriving escapes from boredom. In many instances, boredom might be preferable.

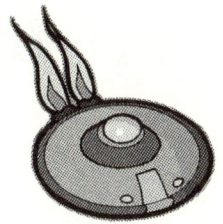

Thirty-four

Sports

For some people the sport they follow (not participate in) is more than just entertainment. It provides experience more satisfying than their job, more meaningful than their religion, more interesting than their families. Sports serve the same function for some men that romantic fiction provides for some women.

The intensity of some fans' loyalty is so strong that they brood when their team loses, exult when it wins, and treat those around them harshly or generously, depending on the results of sporting events. The professional football championship is decided on Superbowl Sunday. And on Superbowl Sunday violent family abuse increases by 40%.

For many people all over the world golf has become the most popular sport, for participants as well as spectators. Hitting a little ball with the proper stick into a little hole in the ground fascinates millions of people. The cost of indulging in this activity is exorbitant in golf courses at famous clubs.

For most American sports fans the foreign frenzy over soccer, which results in riots and killings, seems ridiculous. What is worth getting excited about and cheering and screaming about, is football. In this activity eleven men on each side, some weighing three hundred pounds, push each other around and throw the ball carrier to the ground.

Football used to be a sport but has become a big business.

A sociologist has suggested that the football Superbowl has become the national holiday of the United States.

In the United States, basketball is extremely popular. Throwing a ball into a basket, from a long distance if possible, requires the constant running of five men on each side for sixty minutes.

The players who put the ball into the basket most frequently are rewarded, in professional basketball, with million-dollar salaries, and in amateur basketball with scholarships to college. Basketball used to be a sport but has become a big business.

Crowds at famous auto-races refuse to admit that the likelihood of fatal accidents is one of the attractions. And the men who control professional hockey pretend that fights on the ice do not bring out bigger crowds.

Heavyweight boxing matches pay the largest prizes to the competitors. But everyone denies that the civilized audience is bloodthirsty. Boxing and wrestling express aggression in the most obvious way.

Boxing is a brutal activity, called a sport, in which two human beings hit each other as hard as they can for a specified period of time. In civilized America, successful boxers are paid millions of dollars.

In wrestling men throw each other around and stomp on each other, to the delight of the civilized crowd, male and female. Pacifists can't understand why. Wrestling used to be a sport but it has become a big business.

Some purists say that competitors in Olympic Games should not wear the names of brewers and shoemakers on their uniforms.

The illiteracy of many sports announcers spreads grammatical errors all over the country. "He ran very good," "he done it good," "he seen it," "between he and I" are just a few examples.

Columnist Russell Baker says that in America it is sport rather than religion that is the opiate of the people. And the former owner of a hockey team, Bruce McNall, assumed that the spectators at sports events live vicariously through their heroes, trying to compensate for their own drab, disappointing lives. McNall also believes that the public builds its heroes up, but prefers to bring them down. The fall, he says, is more interesting; that's human nature. He himself went bankrupt shortly after the interview.

A few social scientists have gone so far as to say that sports have assumed some of the characteristics that religion traditionally provided for masses of people. Sports, they say, permit people to identify with something outside of themselves, to share an enthusiasm more volatile than is found in houses of worship, and to transcend for a while the reality of their existence.

Whether this is true or not I cannot, of course, say. But indisputably, sports provide a tremendous outlet for a universal human characteristic—aggression.

Thirty-five

Art Criticism

All symbols in art are interpreted to suit the current wish of the interpreter.

Among pseudo-sophisticated groups the emphasis in art shifts from content to style, from material to method.

The French in particular admire manner excessively and sometimes esteem *how* something is said more that *what* is said.

Society usually admires facetiousness more than wisdom, solving riddles more than solving problems, remembering events more than understanding them.

Chacun a son goût. There is no accounting for people's tastes.

It is hard to understand why some squiggles and splashes of random colors are called modern "art."

In human relations one does not expect perfection. In art, one tries to get it.

Dead critics are harmless critics.

Semioticians claim that every work of art is a symbolic representation of something. Unfortunately, they do not agree on what these deeper meanings are.

A continuing controversy tries to draw a line between legal entertainment and illegal pornography. The term "redeeming social value" has failed to be a satisfactory test.

About many actions and creations one might say: It was well done, but was it worth doing?

Thirty-six

Pop Culture

Gresham's Law explained that bad money drives out good money. Similarly, bad art drives out good art, and low culture drives out all standards of good taste. Modern technology has spread the effects of Gresham's Law all over the art world.

Although only those with IQ's below 100 are technically subnormal, the level of popular culture in the U.S. reveals a much greater number of numskulls.

The defenders of pop culture argue that good taste is an artificial and outmoded concept. Pop culture proves it.

The trick of popular appeal is to express the obvious in a style that makes people think it is original.

American pop culture pervades the world, arousing the fury of the French Academy and of British intellectuals. The rock-and-roll of America pollutes the world's ears.

"Doggerel" used to be the name of an inferior kind of verse. Now it is the most popular rhyme in America and is called "rapping."

Most popular art is trash and most people's aesthetic criteria are banal. They like the obvious, the sentimental, and the gaudy.

Thirty-seven

Epistemology (The Limits of Knowledge)

The motto on Montaigne's seal was *Que sais je?* ("What do I know?") It is a motto all human beings ought to adopt.

The enormous contradictions between popular beliefs (theists vs. atheists, authoritarian vs. libertarians, for example) suggest that some of them may not be totally correct. All *deductive* beliefs are based on their major premises—which are challenged by people who begin with very different premises. All *inductive* beliefs are based on the experiences of different individuals, who have had very different experiences.

Enrico Fermi, the famous Italian physicist, said, "Before hearing this lecture I was confused about this subject. Having heard it, I am still confused, but on a higher plane."

When Albert Einstein said he never believed an axiom, he was offering sound advice to gullible people. But few human beings have taken his counsel.

When emotion conflicts with reason, emotion wins. People believe whatever they want to believe.

Human ignorance is enormous. Thomas Edison, the great American inventor, said, "We don't know one-hundredth of one percent about anything."

The word "true" must often be modified by the question "true for whom?" and "true under which circumstances?"

Most valid new concepts are ridiculed and rejected before they are accepted.

Although no one knows when an event occurs whether it will eventually prove helpful or harmful, people keep making instant faulty judgments about these events.

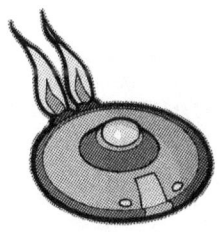

Thirty-eight

Nature of Illusions

Human beings have a great need to create illusions. Many people convince themselves that what they wish to be true is true.

People who see magical visions have a strong desire to see magical visions.

"To me you're a captain, and to you you're a captain. But to captains you are no captain," the mother of a nouveau-riche boat owner told her son.

There is no law to prevent people from believing whatever nonsense they choose to believe.

Napoleon said, "It is by baubles that men are led."

Every nation convinces itself that the wars it wages are just, and the wars its antagonists wage against it are unjust.

No human being is sure of what is illusion and what is reality.

What people call cynicism is often simply the ability to see the world as it is, not as people wish it to be.

Francis Crick, co-discoverer of DNA, said in an interview, "You, your joys and your sorrows, your memories and your ambitions, your sense of personal identity and free will, are in fact no more than the behavior of a vast assembly of nerve cells and their associated molecules."

The newspaper that quoted Crick points out that if he is right, the theory would destroy all accepted concepts of religion, society, soul, or life after death.

Crick's statement has, understandably, failed to achieve much popularity.

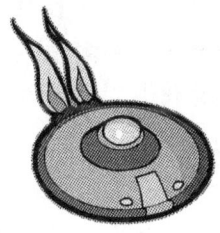

Thirty-nine

Misinformation

When I first landed on the planet Earth I believed everything I heard or read. I was pleased to see on television that spokesmen for large corporations were wishing me, personally, a very merry Christmas. I was touched to hear from advertisers their personal good wishes for my Happy New Year. I was surprised to see that even paper napkins in restaurants were aware of my patronage and thanked me for it. And I was gratified to be told by a sign at the exit of a large store: "Thank you for shopping K-Mart."

But I was quickly disillusioned.

Misinformation—both accidental and intentional—is instantly available in the computer age.

All messages sent by modern communication devices seem equally truthful, even when many of them are in fact distortions of the truth, perversions of the truth, and outright lies.

People believe what they are told to believe, if they are told often enough and simply enough.

Tabloids have the largest circulation of American newspapers—if newspapers they can be called. They thrive on sensationalism, sex, scandal, and absurd myths.

Cultural anthropologist Elizabeth Bird found that tabloids keep repeating, in contemporary form, certain eternal themes of folklore. There is the hero who didn't die (Elvis, John F. Kennedy, Jimmy Hoffa); monsters (Big Foot has superseded dragons); children raised by animals (as Romulus and Remus once were); flying saucers (Carl Jung identified, in medieval paintings, pictures of round objects appearing in the skies), and fairy tales about princes and princesses.

Psychologist Abraham Maslow pointed out that psychiatrists, seeing only disturbed individuals, reach erroneous conclusions about the rest of humanity.

Supposedly rational scholars passionately support the scholars they agree with and vitriolically attack the ones who have different ideas.

Scholars claim that logic is what they rely on, but in fact they are as emotional as everyone else.

Since no Earthling knows the entire truth about any person or any complex event, no one can know the complete truth. When one is informed by the media about individuals or events with which he or she is familiar, one gets a malicious satisfaction out of knowing that parts of the report are false.

As Oscar Wilde pointed out, "Modern journalism, by giving us the opinions of the uneducated, keep us in touch with the ignorance of the community."

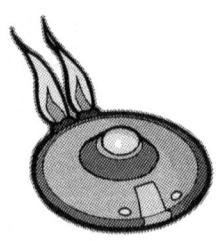

Forty

Wishfulness

Human beings often ignore reason and use instead wish fulfillment devices to provide gratification in their daily lives.

A popular form of wish fulfillment is immortality. The easiest way to achieve a form of immortality is to have something—a place or an object or a procedure or a disease—named after a person. Eponymy immortalizes the discoverers of plants and chemical elements and of new forms of clothing and foods.

George Bernard Shaw suggested that the easiest way of achieving immortality without working is martyrdom. Having something named after you works better and is much less painful.

In Greek mythology Pygmalion carved an ivory statue of a perfect woman and fell in love with it. The Goddess Athena brought the statue to life. Since then many human beings have tried to create perfect objects of love, with less success.

All tales that end with "and they lived happily ever after" are wish-fulfillment devices. As are the highly unlikely happy endings of detective stories, Westerns, adventure tales, and romantic fiction.

It is not an accident that in the most popular fairy tale in the world, Cinderella is rewarded simply for being good—not for possessing any special skill.

Horatio Alger became one of the most popular authors in the U.S. by writing about ordinary people whose goodness was eventually rewarded in very satisfying fashion.

Most Americans receive letters notifying them that they almost won million-dollar prizes in a lottery, and are urged to participate in the next sweepstake. Many Americans continue to take part in this scam.

Human beings utilize a great variety of devices to escape from monotony and disappointment. Besides liquor and drugs and fanaticism there are love potions and patent medicines and gurus.

Wishful thinking is demonstrated by the Hindu bathing in the Ganges River to purify his spirit. And the orthodox Jew going to the river on the annual Day of Atonement to cast away his sins. And the Japanese striking a bell 108 times on New Year's Eve to drive out the 108 sins. And the Catholics' confessional.

Humans wishfully believe in immortality. Among the popular returns after death are the Greek Euridice and Alcestis, ghosts, and Lazarus in the Bible.

For the nostalgic alumnus the performance of his college's athletic teams becomes a major interest in his life, in an attempt to relive a youth that never actually resembled his recollection of it. It is a sad kind of life that needs a college sports team to give it meaning.

The variety of wish-fulfillment devices makes one respect the human imagination.

East Indian folk-tales include several charming wish-fulfillment devices. There is the rabbit that delivers letters. A hat that pays for everything. A wand that revives the dead. Another wand rejuvenates the old. A gold-dropping horse. Trees that grow gold garments and other goodies. And a fishing pole that catches fish and brings them to the house.

In Japan one form of wishful thinking consists of hanging paper prayers on trees and on the walls of temples whose gods are popularly assumed to be particularly amenable to those particular prayers.

Some human observers believe that all illusions are justified, all wish fulfillment devices are necessary. Anything that makes life more bearable, they insist, is a good thing, whether it is true or not. Many people, ordinary, anxious, are stuck in a hopeless rut. What would life be like if they couldn't dream of escapes? Gambling may be good for them, and religions, and sport fantasies, and politics. Truth has nothing to do with it. As a matter of fact, the truth terrifies them or depresses them.

The need for wish fulfillment does not decrease with age. It merely changes. The fairy tales that delight children are no more absurd than adult sexual fantasies, which simply require other forms and other trappings, like the decor of Las Vegas.

The enormous amount of lying, deception, and hypocrisy in the lives of human beings may well be an expression of wishfulness.

Forty-one

Superstition

Although superstition is an irrational belief based on ignorance or fear, an enormous number of intelligent and educated human beings are superstitious.

The three most common superstitions of the Western world are about walking under a ladder, having a black cat cross one's path, and the number thirteen.

Superstitions abound concerning dreams, colors, amulets, charms, talismans, and the luck-bringing qualities of certain gems when matched with certain birth months.

In many "primitive" countries the natives refuse to be photographed because they believe the photograph takes away the soul of the person whose picture is taken. But if paid enough, they pose.

Saying "God bless you" when a person sneezes goes back to ancient Athens, when a sneeze was the first sign that a person had caught the plague.

An old Herefordshire superstition is: If you wear a toad's heart concealed about your person, you can steal without being caught. Modern thieves manage to steal safely without bothering with toads' hearts.

Touching wood is done when announcing good fortune or good health. People who do this are seeking the protection of supernatural beings. Another explanation: At one time sanctuary was granted to a hunted person who managed to touch the wooden door of a church.

Perhaps the most pervasive superstition of modern America is astrology, the belief that the positions of the planets at different times affect the lives of human beings.

Many primitive people believe that it is dangerous to step on a person's shadow.

Some people unlock all doors and windows so that the soul of a dead person is not hindered from departing. The Chinese, I am told, used to make a hole in the roof of the dwelling to facilitate the departure of the soul. They, like everyone else, hope that the departing soul travels upward.

Orthodox Jews cover the mirrors in the homes of the dead.

Niels Bohr, a famous physicist, explained why there was a horseshoe hanging on his wall: "Of course I don't believe in it. But I understand that it brings you luck whether you believe in it or not."

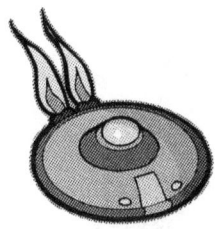

Forty-two

Fashion

In the United States fashion changes continually in clothing, the arts, politics, entertainment, automobiles, and public opinion.

Usually "fashions" originate among the famous, prominent, or wealthy, and seep down to the masses. American economist Thorstein Veblen described fashion as a form of "conspicuous consumption," an attempt to show the public that one can afford to buy the latest products simply because they are currently popular. In industrialized societies fashions flourish because they provide an easy means for people to display, or to simulate, financial success.

Another form of peculiar mass behavior is the "fad," a temporary fashion or manner of action that sweeps the country, then quickly disappears. The popularity of these silly fads is hard to explain, as the history of pet rocks and streaking demonstrates.

Women's fashions sometimes exaggerate buttocks, sometimes try to hide them; sometimes expose breasts, sometimes cover them. Fashions reflect the morals of the time, or the aesthetics of the time, always the pretensions of the time. Women with attractive legs wear short skirts or shorts. The others wear slacks.

Although clothing was originally intended to provide warmth and protection, that purpose has been long forgotten. Now clothes constrict or display, sometimes retaining elements serving a long outdated need—such as the buttons on the sleeves of King Frederick's soldiers that discouraged wiping one's nose on one's sleeves. These buttons still appear on men's coat sleeves.

"What has been the fashion once will come into fashion again," says a Japanese proverb.

There is now a custom in the United States of issuing annual lists of what is "in" and what is "out" for the coming year. These lists tell a gullible public what entertainers, foods, fads, and politicians are currently in popular favor and which individuals, objects, and activities are passe.

Almost all of these items are trivial. But human beings need trivia. They cannot be expected to spend all their time speculating about metaphysics and teleology. They do have a need for constant chatter. The superficial and the trivial satisfy this need.

Men pretend that they are much more rational than women about changes in fashion. The width of a tie, the angle of a lapel, the color of a stripe, these significant details are carefully evaluated each season by the fashion-conscious male—and then accepted.

When women attend sales that offer genuine bargains they buy things whether they are fashionable or not, if the price is low enough.

Oscar Wilde put it succinctly: "Fashion is a form of ugliness so intolerable that we have to alter it every six months."

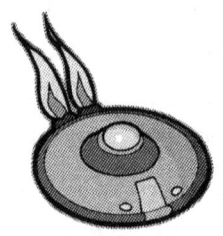

Forty-three

History

In attempts to find a pattern in human history scholars have offered a number of theories. Their explanations are interesting, persuasive—and contradictory. Some sages believe that "great men" make history—just as Plutarch and Ralph Waldo Emerson and Harry Truman maintained. Other scholars reached the opposite conclusion. They believe the "conditions of society" permit fortunate individuals, who happen to be living in certain places at certain times, to become "great" men.

Historian Arnold Toynbee insisted that a "creative minority" of superior men determined the course of history. But most modern historians believe that it is social forces that determine what happens to nations.

In spite of claims to objectivity, all accounts of human history depend on what individual of what nation is writing the account.

A number of scholars discovered, or thought they discovered, that there are cycles in history. Unfortunately, the cycles each scholar identified are different from the cycles that other scholars identified.

It is "economic determinism" that shapes history, insists Karl Marx. No, it is "social evolution" that directs humanity's inevitable progression to perfection, Herbert Spencer declared. "Civilization," Spencer wrote, "is a progress from indefinite, incoherent homogeneity toward a coherent heterogeneity." History is purposeful, guided by divine will, claim theologians of several major religions. History is purposeless, Leo Tolstoy tried to show in *War and Peace*. There is a synthesis of thesis and antithesis in history, Hegel proved to his own satisfaction, if not to everyone else's.

It appears to a detached observer like myself that with so many conflicting theories of history available, anyone who insists that only his or her theory of history is correct may be guilty of excessive egotism at best, conscious hypocrisy at worst. There is no law, of course, prohibiting a scholar from having both of these defects at the same time.

It would be difficult to make a romantic tale out of the ancient Greeks' economic reasons for attacking Troy, or of the Queen of Sheba's commerce-arranging visit to Jerusalem. So history was conveniently rewritten, inventing the elopement of Helen and the sexual interest of King Solomon.

The twentieth century was the century in which greater concern for the poor, the weak, and the sick was shown in the Western world than ever before. This was also the century in which more people were slaughtered in genocides, pogroms, "ethnic cleansings," and wars than in any previous century.

During the twentieth century the most highly educated countries in their parts of the world, Germany and Japan, proved to be the most bellicose, the most brutal, and the most immoral. Is there a clue here that I failed to notice?

Russian-born American novelist Ayn Rand was less than reverent in her accusation: "Every major horror of history was committed in the name of an altruistic motive."

French Prime Minister Georges Clemenceau wrote, "America is the only nation in history which miraculously has gone directly from barbarism into degeneration without the usual interval of civilization."

As to the lessons of history, the German philosopher Hegel concluded, "What experience and history teaches is this—people and governments have never learned anything from history, or acted on principles derived from history." The American philosopher George Santayana agreed: "Men who forget their history are doomed to relive it."

None of this advice has had the slightest influence on the behavior of human beings.

Forty-four

Philosophy

It is a rash statement for an extraterrestrial visitor like me to make, but my reading of philosophers convinces me that every human philosopher has created an elaborate rationalization to satisfy the needs of his own temperament. Each philosopher sees the world from the perspective of his or her own experience, and evaluates the world in terms of his or her own personality. But they all pretend that their view of the world is a universal vision.

A century ago an English scholar, John Churchill Collins, wrote, "Truth is the object of philosophy, but not always of philosophers." He was right then, and he is right now. Plato and Berkeley thought they proved the validity of Idealism, and Democritus and Hobbes thought that they proved the validity of Materialism. But Idealism and Materialism contradict each other.

All major systems of philosophy are confuted by other major systems of philosophy; they all depend on the premises with which they begin. And premises that seem undeniable to some people seem absurd to others. It is not the correctness of their ideas but their skill in presenting those ideas that establishes persons as philosophers.

Philosophers and lawyers use "logic" as a major tool in their trades. But no one knows better than philosophers and lawyers that they can use logic to reach opposite conclusions.

Dialectic is defined as the art of logical argumentation. But philosophers have made of dialectic the art of illogical argumentation.

There are many ways for Earthlings to play rhetorical tricks, such as false dilemmas: "Have you stopped beating your wife? Answer yes or no." "Heads I win, tails you lose." "Do you agree with me or are you a moron?"

Also, in philosophy there are many examples of famous, but unconvincing, reasoning. "Let us assume that certain things are true. Therefore, they are true," argued German philosopher Immanuel Kant. "I think, therefore I am," said French philosopher René Descartes. (He might as easily have said: "I sneeze, therefore I am.")

Ideas have actual form, announced Greek philosopher Plato. God is dead, German philosopher Friedrich Nietzsche told the world. God is absent, but I am here, said French philosopher Jean-Paul Sartre. There are many more of these gems.

Some people believe that all values are absolute, some believe they are all relative, and some believe that there are both absolute values and relative values. Convincing arguments have been made by philosophers for all three positions.

Recent discoveries in neurobiology challenge all previous assumptions about the nature of morality. The journal *Science* reports that in the prefrontal cortex of the brain there is a location where a person's moral judgments are made. When this part of the brain is affected by physical injury or a genetic defect, the individual becomes incapable of making ethical decisions.

This does not solve all problems. It is unlikely that all the ordinary people who carried out atrocities under orders were psychopaths. And, ostensibly, the greatest source of morality is religion. The Inquisitors in Spain who burned heretics at the stake may have lacked a moral gene. They did not lack firewood. The ordinary human beings in Nazi Germany who carried out the Holocaust may have had normal cortices. They also knew how to operate gas chambers.

It is revealing, and for human students of philosophy somewhat disillusioning, that Bertrand Russell, who co-authored the most important text on logic in the twentieth century, concluded: "Philosophy is an unusually ingenious attempt to think fallaciously."

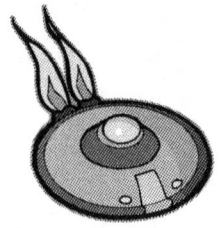

Forty-five

Psychology

Human psychologists do not understand psychology well enough to predict what any human being will do. Neither does anyone else.

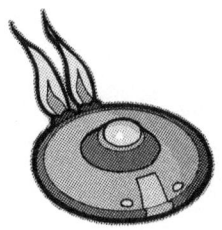

Forty-six

Religion

All religions are based on unverifiable claims. For believers, the unprovable is immune to disproof.

Christianity is the worship of Jehovah and Jesus Christ by people who pretend to practice the teachings of Jehovah and Jesus Christ.

Judaism is the worship of Jehovah by people who pretend to practice the teachings of Jehovah.

Islam is the worship of Allah by people who pretend to practice the teachings of Allah.

Hinduism is the worship of 5,000 gods, more or less, by people who pretend to practice the teachings of some of these gods.

Buddhism is the worship of Buddha, who taught that he was not God and should not be worshipped.

Capitalism is the worship of money by people who pretend that they do not worship money.

Communism is the worship of equality by people who pretend that they practice equality.

According to Judeo-Christian mythology, Adam was the first man, whose wife's unfortunate choice of fruits is the source of all human misery.

Many cultures do not believe the Eden myth and do not feel guilty about eating forbidden fruit. But these cultures have found something else about which they feel guilty. Or, like the Japanese, they have substituted shame for guilt as a basic ingredient of their culture.

Surprisingly, the Bible makes silviculture the source of ethics. Neither Adam nor Eve knew anything about good and evil until they tasted a fruit from the Tree of Knowledge.

An ancient myth insists that what Satan showed Eve was not fruit but his penis. A logical myth, since women have always shown more interest in penises than in fruits.

In writing the story of creation in Genesis the scribes mixed two previous myths, one Babylonian and the other Canaanite. Good secretarial help was hard to find, even in those days.

Some scholars claim that Abraham, Isaac, and Jacob are not the names of persons but are generic names of wandering tribes. Individuals are more interesting to read about than groups.

Long before Moses was described as an abandoned infant, a divider of ocean waters, and the possessor of a magic ring, earlier myths attributed all those experiences to earlier heroes.

A book recently published in the U.S. lists the total number of angels, their names, and their special talents. The author's sources do not seem to be completely reliable.

"We never do evil so completely and cheerfully as when we do it for religious reasons," said French philosopher Blaise Pascal. A man as religious as Pascal should know.

Prophets often mistake their own desires for God's will.

Every action is excusable if the perpetrator claims divine sanction. During the war with Vietnam some American soldiers coined the slogan, "Kill a Commie for Christ."

Most religions provide official justification for the actions of their countries, right or wrong.

In Tahiti certain priests dig holes into which the sins of rich dying men are buried. Rich Westerners should consider this procedure.

If you use Abraham Lincoln's reasoning—"God must love the common man; he made so many of them"—you could also say, "God must love cancer; he made so much of it."

If God keeps track of every human action he requires an enormous system of bookkeeping. With computers the job should be easier.

Fairness is one gift God never promised.

A creationist is a person who believes that the Earth was literally created in six days. Archeologists and geologists do not support such a time frame.

There are many ways of interpreting divine commands, depending on the interpreter.

In the Old Testament priests are indifferent to the slaughter of human beings but violently indignant over methods of slaughtering cows and chickens.

It is as easy to get intoxicated on religion as on other stimulants.

In Deuteronomy (in the Old Testament) there are sixty-four verses of curses and only fourteen verses of blessings.

The biggest problem in Heaven, Mark Twain suspected, may be boredom.

Many clergy are people who have simply gone into the religion business instead of some other business.

As Americans move up in the class system they tend to adopt a higher-ranking religious denomination.

It is not easy for devout Jews to explain why God permitted His chosen people to suffer the Holocaust.

When tornadoes demolish churches, and earthquakes kill the occupants of a mosque, religious people have trouble explaining the reason for the catastrophe. The destruction of synagogues can usually be accounted for more simply.

In cold Tibet, Hell is described as a very cold place.

Catholics reserve the lowest level of Hell for suicides. Japanese reserve the highest level of Heaven for the proper kind of suicide.

In almost every culture the idea of death is so frightening that the local belief-system concocts some notion of "afterlife" to encourage the living. It's a winning proposition. The dead are in no condition to report.

One of the strategies human beings have devised for facing the inevitability of death is the hope that the soul is immortal.

Another human strategy for accepting the inconvenience of dying is the notion of reincarnation. After a series of reincarnations the average soul must be very tired of the itinerary.

American attitudes toward religion are sometimes revealed by unexpected sources, as in the following graffiti:

"God is not dead. He just doesn't want to get involved." "The Lord giveth, and the Lord taketh away. The Lord is an Indian giver." "God grades on a curve."

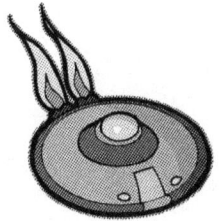

Forty-seven

Positive Qualities

At first glance it may seem that the negative characteristics of human beings are predominant. The history of wars, persecutions, ethnic hatreds, and religious pogroms offers strong evidence of human viciousness. And that's only counting group activity.

But, perversely, there is another side to the human personality. People do "good" things as well as "bad" ones. History shows love and generosity and courage and incredibly noble behavior. Human beings sometimes risk their own lives to prevent others from dying in fires and floods and wars. In view of what I said before, these statements are hard to believe. Nevertheless, they are true.

In animal society the permanent tension between hunger and satiety results in what Charles Darwin called "survival of the fittest." But human beings who reject the concept of "Social Darwinism" (the concept applied to humankind) list the following items in defense of humanity.
1. Help by individuals to the old, sick, handicapped, poor, and victimized.
2. Help by institutions to the above.
3. Laws intended to protect the weak and minorities.
4. The idea of freedom.
5. The belief in equality.
6. Sporadic (and often self-serving) applications of benevolent religious teachings.
7. Attempts at international cooperation, such as the United Nations.
8. The use of aggression, by some individuals and some institutions, on behalf of "good" causes and socially desirable conditions.

There are human beings with an enormous zest for life. They face each challenge as an adventure and each encounter as a gratifying experience. There are people who love the work they are doing and feel that it is both personally satisfying and useful to society. There are men and women who find constant fulfillment in helping others and improving the larger community. There are good people who are also happy people. It's a pity that there are not more of them.

Also, idealism and spirituality exist, as surely as selfishness and materialism. One cannot deny the presence of positive behavior any more than one can ignore the effects of negative action.

Human beings seem to possess the potential for goodness, even when they fail to develop it. Above the level of subsistence, people make choices. As long as doing good does not hurt a person economically, or socially, he or she is as likely to behave well as to behave badly.

Finally, I have observed among Earthlings a phenomenon sadly missing on our planet. It is called love, and it has many manifestations. One form is a strong affection for another human being. People who develop this affection find life much more satisfying. They support each other, share experiences, comfort one another, and trust one another. Many couples I have watched, families I have observed, and individuals I have met, love and are loved. It is the most endearing quality of Earthlings that I have seen.

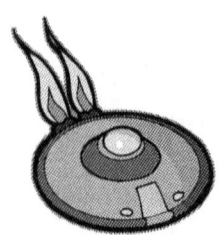

Forty-eight

Conclusion

I am not a cynic—I'm a realist. And this is what I've learned about life on Earth.

On Earth the perception of reality is as important as reality itself. If a person thinks that light is good and dark is bad, he or she takes action in accordance with that attitude. Similarly, people who believe in heaven and hell may, like people who believe in dieting, modify their behavior. Accepting preposterous myths does not seem to disturb Earthlings in the least.

Human beings find negative behavior much more interesting than positive action. In television and radio news, in popular newspapers and magazines and books, in films and videos, it is the depiction of misbehavior and crime and catastrophe that stimulates sales. Violence, conflict, accidents, fires, aberrant sexual behavior—all these seem to fascinate human beings.

The quiet, peaceful aspects of daily life, the loving families and well-adjusted people seem to bore readers and viewers and listeners. Decency and happiness are not newsworthy or film-worthy. The visitor to Earth who relies on the popular media for an accurate view of human society will be seriously misled.

Perhaps the most important warning that the extraterrestrial visitor must be given is that human society is permeated with deception. Governments lie, institutions lie, individuals lie. What makes the situation more difficult is that they do not lie all the time. Sometimes they tell the truth.

In a pessimistic moment the German writer Goethe wrote, "Our planet is the mental asylum of the universe." He was wrong. A planet in our galaxy named Utopia serves that purpose.

And Aldous Huxley speculated, "Maybe this world is another planet's hell." He too was wrong. In the United States, poverty is hell.

I prefer to end on a less gloomy note. An anonymous scholar told me, "Happiness on Earth consists of finding a satisfying illusion and holding on to it."

Interested in other books published by Pilgrims' Process, Inc.? Remove this page, fill out the form below, fold on the dotted line, tape closed, attach a postage stamp, and drop it in the mail. We will keep you informed about our publications.

Name: _____

Address: _____

City: _____ State: _____

ZIP: _____

E-mail address: _____

I am particularly interested in publications on:

- -

Pilgrims' Process, Inc.
4657 Huey Circle
Boulder, CO 80305-6736

☐

Pilgrims' Process, Inc.
4657 Huey Circle
Boulder, CO 80305-6736

Hyprocisy
Don't Leave Home Without It

by

Leonard Feinberg

You've read **The ET Visitor's Guide to the U.S.A.,** now read the research behind it.

"Some things about hypocrisy are well known. First, it has a very long history. In the scriptures of all great religions and in the literatures of ancient civilizations there are many references to hypocrites. Secondly, hypocrisy is universal. Proverbs, folk tales, and written records all over the world provide ample evidence of hypocritical behavior. Thirdly, hypocrisy is pervasive. It is practiced by individuals and institutions at every level of society." (From the conclusion of *Hyprocisy*.)

Forthcoming in 2002 from Pilgrims' Process, Inc.

Following the Milky Way: A Pilgrimage on the Camino de Santiago, 2nd edition

Elyn Aviva

Whether you are a spiritual seeker, an avid outdoor adventurer, or an armchair traveler, you will find this a compelling account of a journey that is as old as human longing and as modern as tomorrow.

Following the Milky Way is the story of Elyn Aviva's first 500-mile-long journey on foot on the Camino de Santiago. This 1000-year-old pilgrimage road stretches from the French Pyrenees across northern Spain to Santiago de Compostela, supposed tomb of St. James the Apostle. It is a journey that crosses the landscape of the soul as well as the mountains and mesetas of Spain.

This book is a vivid memoir of a life-changing adventure, chance encounters, unforeseen dangers, and unexpected pleasures. Spanish history, wine, food, literature, art, architecture, and legend share equal time with the stories of pilgrims that Elyn meets along the way. *Following the Milky Way* is a fascinating historical document. Today, hundreds of thousands of people—including Shirley MacLaine—are going on the Camino, but *Following the Milky Way* describes the pilgrimage in 1982, when the Camino was nearly abandoned.

This second edition includes a new introduction that explores the meaning of pilgrimage in greater detail, delves more deeply into the esoteric symbols and pre-Christian shrines that lie hidden within the Way, and provides a unique look at the changes that have occurred in the pilgrimage in recent years.

Pilgrims' Process, Inc.
4657 Huey Circle
Boulder, CO 80305-6736
Peregrino@aol.com

320 pp   ISBN   0-9710609-0-8

Dead End on the Camino:
A Noa Webster Mystery

Elyn Aviva

Murder, mayhem, and mystery accompany anthropologist Noa Webster on her treasure hunt on the Camino de Santiago.

While doing research in the National Library in Madrid, Noa accidentally discovers a baffling, 500-year-old letter that describes a treasure hidden somewhere on the Camino de Santiago, an ancient pilgrimage road. Impetuously, she embarks on a dangerous quest in which she must use all her wits to decipher clues and find the treasure—and to determine who's a friend and who's a foe. After all, her life depends on it.

Joining her on the hunt are the charming but mercurial Jack Merlot; the tarnished Southern belle Sue Ellen; Noa's sometimes-boyfriend, Peter Murphy; and an assortment of other characters, including men in white robes who mysteriously appear and disappear.

This is the story of a modern adventure inextricably tied to the past. Filled with accurate historical detail, cultural tidbits, and vivid descriptions of culinary delights, cathedrals, and the cities and villages along the Camino, *Dead End on the Camino* takes the reader on a rollicking ride across Spain.

Pilgrims' Process, Inc.
4657 Huey Circle
Boulder, CO 80305-6736
Peregrino@aol.com
224 pp   ISBN   0-9710609-1-6

"Treasure hunt, pleasure read—Dead End was entertaining and educational at the same time. A first-rate mystery that I could not put down until the end!" S.H.

"I never knew what was going to happen, but I never felt lost or confused. And I loved the characters." C.K.

When Aloha Means Goodbye:
A Noa Webster Mystery

Elyn Aviva

Noa Webster is planning to have a relaxing Christmas vacation on the tropical island paradise of Maui. But there's a snake—at least one, possibly more—hiding in the garden. Soon she is catapulted into a desperate search for stolen artifacts as she tries to unravel a tangled web of deceit, passion, and jealousy. Suspected by the police, suspicious of strangers who offer assistance, she must choose her confidantes as carefully as she chooses her words.

Characters include:

Noa Webster, an assistant professor of anthropology at a small New York university. Learns the hard way that things and people are often not what they seem—especially in paradise.

Alex James Cook: Golden haired, golden tongued playboy who claims to be a professional tennis player. Says he's recovering from a broken heart, but it wasn't his heart that killed him.

Ancient sacred carvings stolen from a museum: who stole them, where are they, and to whom do they *really* belong?

David Kukuilani: Hawaiian kahuna who believes that the punishment should fit the crime. Willing to die for what he believes in, but is he also willing to kill for it? Grandfather of the beautiful Melemele.

Melemele Kaohu: Graceful as a gently swaying palm tree, sulky as the sky before a storm.

Bill Miller: A dealer in rare art objects. Suave, refined, but definitely dangerous. Would his desire to "make a killing" lead him to kill?

Richard Wiley: An anthropologist acquaintance of Noa's who just happens to be working with David Kukuilani. What's *his* interest in Noa?

Instead of going sightseeing, Noa finds herself evading would-be kidnappers, dodging bullets, getting a crash course in native Hawaiian rights and rituals, and frantically trying to figure out who did what to whom and why. And she better figure it out fast.

Forthcoming in 2002 from Pilgrims' Process, Inc.

Seeking the Sacred: A Pilgrimage to Mysterious Places and Sacred Sites

Elyn Aviva

Elyn is a seeker of the sacred who has spent the last twenty years traveling pilgrimage roads and experiencing sacred sites. As an anthropologist, she knows how to do research and analyze, and this training adds richness and depth to these essays. As a spiritual seeker, however, Elyn knows that academic inquiry is only one of many ways to experience the sacred.

This collection of travel essays provides a unique combination of first-hand anthropological observation with a pilgrim's appreciation for the holy. Elyn weaves together

- Black Madonnas
- the hidden meanings of the Camino de Santiago
- labyrinth walking in Chartres cathedral and elsewhere
- ancient goddess sites
- the cult of the bulls in Crete, Spain, and southern France
- the mysterious goose foot symbol
- the Grail quest
- whirling dervishes in Turkey

into a fascinating tapestry of overlapping journeys. Some of these essays were previously published in abridged form as magazine articles.

Forthcoming in 2002 from Pilgrims' Process, Inc.

www.ingramcontent.com/pod-product-compliance
Lightning Source LLC
Chambersburg PA
CBHW051802040426
42446CB00007B/478